What Would

Jesus Say

about

Christianity?

From the Heart of Jesus, vol 8

What Would Jesus Say about Christianity?

KIM MICHAELS

Copyright © 2014 Kim Michaels. All rights reserved. No part of this book may be used, reproduced, translated, electronically stored or transmitted by any means except by written permission from the publisher. A reviewer may quote brief passages in a review.

MORE TO LIFE PUBLISHING

www.morepublish.com

For foreign and translation rights,

contact info@ morepublish.com

ISBN: 978-9949-9215-518-61-6

Series ISBN: 978-9949-518-21-0

The information and insights in this book should not be considered as a form of therapy, advice, direction, diagnosis, and/or treatment of any kind. This information is not a substitute for medical, psychological, or other professional advice, counseling and care. All matters pertaining to your individual health should be supervised by a physician or appropriate health-care practitioner. No guarantee is made by the author or the publisher that the practices described in this book will yield successful results for anyone at any time. They are presented for informational purposes only, as the practice and proof rests with the individual.

For more information: *www.askrealjesus.com*

CONTENTS

Introduction: The Problem with Words 9
1 | How Christianity Causes People to Reject Jesus 15
2 | Has Christianity Turned Jesus into Anti-christ? 25
3 | How the Power Elite Destroyed Jesus' Example 39
4 | Peter Represented the Satanic Consciousness 51
5 | The Satanic Foundation of the Catholic Church 65
6 | The Inner Meaning of the Fall of Man 75
7 | Can Christianity Fill People's Spiritual Needs? 85
8 | Christianity Perverted the Concept of a Savior 95
9 | Christianity Has Taken away Jesus' Victory 103
10 | Exposing the Consciousness of Anti-christ 121
11 | How Dark Forces Control Christianity 129
12 | How to Free Christianity from Anti-Christ 145
13 | How Grace and Works Work Together 165
14 | The Force-Based Mindset in Christianity 179
15 | The Suppression of Women in Christianity 187
16 | A Movement Guided by the Spirit 197

INTRODUCTION: THE PROBLEM WITH WORDS

I am a spiritual teacher. I am sent to earth to set human beings free. What is the greatest challenge I face as a spiritual teacher? It is this: The very condition from which you need to be set free prevents you from truly hearing my message. The very condition from which you need to be set free prevents you from hearing the message that can set you free.

Rejecting the ideas that could set us free

The minds of most human beings on earth have become closed systems in which their own circular logic prevents them from hearing the message of a spiritual teacher who can set them free from their self-created, self-sustained mental prisons. Consider how easy it is for people to reject any new idea that comes to them. Consider what people do to reject a new idea. They use some kind of condition that they have defined in their own minds to reject the new idea.

Consider how, around the world, you have groups of people who are basing their outlook on life on a specific thought or belief system, defined by what they see as an ultimate authority. Anytime a new idea is presented to them, they instantly compare the idea to their thought system. Does it validate their thought system? Does it go beyond or even challenge their thought system? If the latter is the case, then they immediately have a seemingly watertight argument for rejecting the new idea.

Why are you still on earth? Why is the earth, still filled with conflict and struggle between human beings? Could it be because human beings have not been willing to look beyond the mental boxes defined by their thought systems? Could it be that human beings have become closed systems who are rejecting the very ideas that could set them free from the struggle and the conflict?

New ideas must come from outside existing systems

What could potentially set human beings free from the struggle and conflict that has been ongoing for thousands of years of recorded history? What might set the captives free? Would it not have to be a new idea? Would not a new idea have to be something that is outside of the existing thought systems found on this planet?

If we are willing to be honest, we will have to recognize — will we not — that the thought systems that exist on planet earth have *not* been able to bring peace and harmony. They have not been able to *end* the struggle. They have, in fact, only *reinforced* the struggle.

If there is to be an end to the struggle, this can come about only when people begin to accept ideas that come from *outside* the mental boxes defined by existing thought systems. If people use their existing thought systems to reject such ideas, how shall they ever be free? How shall there ever be change on earth? How shall there ever be peace?

Consider the problem with words

Consider the fact that what you are reading here is a series of words. Consider that words have different meanings to different people. Just look at any religious scripture found on earth. Those who adhere to that scripture believe it was given by some ultimate authority, and in its original form it had some superior status. Different groups of people have taken the same words and interpreted them very differently, giving them very different meanings. You can see groups of people who are in conflict with each other even though they base their thought systems upon the very same words.

Consider, if you will, that it is possible to interpret words so that they validate *any* viewpoint or belief that you want. If you are willing to use words selectively, you can prove almost anything you want, and this is why people are in conflict. Look at how easy it is for people to take any statement made with words and instantly find a watertight excuse from their thought system for rejecting that statement.

Rejection based on words

Take my opening statement: "I am a spiritual teacher." Consider how many millions of people around the earth would instantly reject that statement. According to their thought system, there is no such thing as a spiritual teacher. They say that there is no such thing as a spiritual realm beyond the material world. The material world is all there is, and all talk of some spiritual realm beyond it is just superstition and nonsense. If there is no spiritual realm beyond the material, how could there be a spiritual teacher in that realm seeking to liberate human beings?

There are even those who would say that human beings do not need to be liberated. There is no higher condition than what they have right now for all of your thoughts, beliefs and impressions of life are just the result of chemical reactions in your brain.

Any statement spoken in words can easily be rejected by either interpreting the words or by using some thought system also defined in words. By considering this, you might realize that there is no such thing as an ultimate statement made with words. Any statement made with words can be interpreted differently by different people. People can accept the statement or reject the statement by using words from their existing thought system. This is precisely the mechanism that limits the ability of a spiritual teacher to liberate people from their own mental boxes.

The mind can reach beyond the material realm

Consider what happens when I tell you more about myself. Consider how – whenever I make a statement about myself – you will instantly compare that statement to your existing thought system and you will use it to accept or reject my statement.

I am a spiritual teacher. I am sent to liberate people on earth. I exist right now in a realm that is beyond the material frequency spectrum, the material level of energies. I exist as a mind that is beyond what you can fathom as a human being. I am speaking to you through a human being who realizes that he is only a human being because he has not yet ascended to the spiritual realm. He acknowledges that the human mind has an ability to tune in to different levels of vibration.

Most human beings on earth spend all of their lives having their minds attuned only to the material frequency spectrum. Some human beings, in fact a considerable number of human beings, have used their mind's ability to turn the dial of consciousness and attune to different frequency spectra beyond the material. Throughout the ages, some people have been able to

Introduction: The Problem with Words

turn the dial of consciousness and attune to the spiritual realm, receiving various forms of messages and ideas, even sometimes spoken messages, from beings in the higher realms. Such messengers have always existed and they have been the originators of a variety of spiritual, even practical, teachings given to humankind from the spiritual realm.

I am one of the spiritual teachers assigned to work with the people embodying on planet earth. As part of my assignment, I once took embodiment, I took incarnation, on earth. The spiritual being that I am entered into a dense physical body like the one you are now wearing. Through that process, I qualified for my permanent ascension into the spiritual realm and that is why I am now an ascended being, an ascended master. I use the term "ascended master" because it signifies that I am ascended and that I ascended by mastering my own mind and thereby attaining the mastery of mind over matter, allowing me to ascend from the matter realm.

All of the statements I have made can be readily invalidated by most of the thought and belief systems currently found on earth. You will see that my statements, made so far, have already formed a filter that has filtered out many human beings. If they have started reading this book, they have already decided with their outer minds that they must reject it because the statements made here go too far beyond their existing thought system and they are not willing to question that thought system. They are not willing to consider, seriously consider, ideas that go beyond that thought system.

How will you ever be free if you are not willing to consider ideas that are beyond your current thought system? It is precisely your current thought system that defines the limitations from which you need to be set free. Again, here is a statement that many people will reject because they firmly believe that their current thought system is the key to their liberation, however they define that liberation.

What I have said up until this point has already filtered out many people, but now I will make a statement that will filter out many more people. I simply ask you to watch your reactions.

When I was in embodiment on earth, I was known as the person named Jesus. I am now the Ascended Master Jesus Christ. If you are still reading these words, notice how my last statement caused a reaction in you. Will you instantly reject this book, or are you willing to let me give you the ideas that can set you free?

1 | HOW CHRISTIANITY CAUSES PEOPLE TO REJECT JESUS

Why do people reject me, the ascended Jesus? We can talk about several groups of people who are predisposed to reject me as an ascended being or reject that I could give a message through a human being.

There are many people who have *not* grown up in a Christian environment and who have been predisposed to reject me, the Ascended Master Jesus Christ. They reject me because of their reaction to the outer religion that claims to represent me on earth. They have been exposed to various aspects of Christianity that they feel in their hearts are not right. They tend to reject me as an ascended being because of the outer organization that claims to represent me.

Yet, *I am* an ascended being. You ascend by transcending *everything* on earth. There is no outer organization or outer teaching that can completely and accurately represent an ascended being. I am a Spirit, and as I said 2,000 years ago: "God is a Spirit and they that worship him must worship him in spirit and in truth." The essential quality of spirit is that it cannot be confined to words. If you use a thought system defined by words to reject the spirit, you have lost the spirit. You will never know the Spirit that I am if you reject me because of what you have been exposed to by an outer organization on earth.

There are also people who have grown up in a Christian environment, and they have also been exposed to various things from the Christian religion that they feel conflict what they know to be real and true in their hearts. They have looked for other types of spiritual teachings or perhaps they have rejected *all* spiritual teachings. Many of these people are actually open to new ideas, but they are not open to *me,* the Ascended Master Jesus Christ. They reject everything that sounds like a Christian religion, and they have not been willing or able to separate Christ from Christianity. They have not been willing to realize that I – as a spiritual being, as an ascended being – am *more* than the image of me presented by the Christian religion.

Of course, we have more than one billion people on this earth who call themselves Christians and who claim to be followers of Jesus Christ. How will *they* react when they read in a book a message from a being who claims to be the real, ascended Jesus Christ? Most of them will instantly reject that statement, and they will use their own thought system to reject it.

The irony that Christians are the first to reject Jesus

Do you possibly see the irony here? The very people who claim to be the true followers of Jesus Christ are the first ones to reject a statement from the real, ascended Jesus Christ. Right here, you see one of my purposes for bringing forth this book. Right here, you see one of the major problems I have with the Christian religion.

I am the real, ascended Jesus Christ! It is my intent with this book to put forth a statement of what I, as an ascended being in this particular time, think about the Christian religion that claims to represent me on earth.

1 | How Christianity Causes People to Reject Jesus

The greatest problem I have for giving this statement is that the very people who claim to be my true followers will be the first ones to reject my statement. They will even reject my very existence as an ascended being who could possibly speak to human beings without going through their particular church and the authority and power structure of that church.

Why is this so ironical? It is ironical because the very people who rejected me when I walked the earth 2,000 years ago also were the ones who thought they were the true followers of the only true religion.

So many of the Jews in Israel rejected me. Almost all of the scribes and Pharisees and the other authority figures in the Jewish religion rejected me. They rejected me because I brought forth ideas and statements that challenged the mental box of their religion.

I had come to set the captives free. How can I set you free if I do not challenge your mental box? It is precisely your mental box that keeps you trapped on earth and prevents you from entering the kingdom of God. Where is the kingdom of God to be found? Did I not say, 2,000 years ago, that the kingdom does not come with the observation of an outer religion for the kingdom of God is within you? *The kingdom of God is a state of consciousness.*

Liberation from the illusion of separation

The reason human beings on earth – all human beings, Christians or not – need to be liberated is that they are trapped in a lower state of consciousness in which they believe in the illusion that they are separated from God and God's kingdom. You need to be liberated from the *illusion* of separation. In order for that liberation to occur, you must be willing to challenge the very beliefs and illusions that make up the mental box that causes you to identify yourself as a being who is separated from your source, from your Father's kingdom.

If the kingdom of God is within you, how can you be separated from that kingdom in reality? Only in your mind can there be the illusion that you are separated from the kingdom, and it is *this* illusion from which you need to be liberated. How can you be liberated from the illusion of separation unless some spiritual teacher – who is not trapped in this illusion – comes to you and challenges the illusion? If you use the illusion to reject the teacher sent to set you free, how can you ever be liberated?

You may think the world has changed a lot in these past 2,000 years, but I tell you: The very central psycho-spiritual dynamic that keeps human beings trapped in a lower state of consciousness is exactly the same today as it was 2,000 years ago. Most people have a wider, more encompassing mental box than people had 2,000 years ago, but they are still trapped by their mental boxes and they need to be liberated from them.

There is only one way to be liberated from a mental box and that is to have someone, who is not inside the box, come to you and give you a statement – that you can hear or read – that challenges your mental box. Why did I take incarnation 2,000 years ago? Because only by being in a physical body could I make statements that people could actually hear!

The problem was that people could hear my words with their outer minds, but they did not truly hear the message behind the words with their hearts. Their hearts were closed by the outer mind's attachment to particular beliefs and thought systems. This is no different today than it was back then.

Why Jesus cannot come back

There is a cosmic law that made it possible for me to take incarnation on earth in the capacity of the Living Christ. This law also means that I could only do this once. I cannot come back into embodiment today, regardless of what some Christian churches believe or regardless of the fact that some misguided individuals claim to be Jesus Christ come again. I am an *ascended* being, I am not coming back into a physical body or any other physical apparition. My only option today is to give messages from the ascended realm through messengers who have been willing to turn the dial of consciousness and tune in to my Spirit, the Spirit that I AM.

The difficulty in this process is that I am a *spiritual* being. In the spiritual realm we do not communicate through words. We have a higher, non-verbal form of communication. Through this non-verbal communication we are able to communicate a message that has much greater wholeness than what can be communicated through words on earth. Precisely because human beings are trapped in a certain mental box, most human beings are not able to grasp non-verbal communication. Most human beings think in words, they even label their feelings by using words. As a spiritual being, my only potential for reaching most people is to communicate through words. I can do this through a messenger who has been willing to be trained to turn the dial of consciousness and tune in to my Spirit.

As soon as my non-verbal message is translated into words, people can use their existing thought system to reject those words. They have seemingly watertight, authoritative reasons for rejecting these words, as you might notice that your mind can come up with many reasons for rejecting the words you have read so far.

"Can this really be the real Jesus Christ, speaking through a human messenger, giving forth these words? Can these words really be accurate? Can they really be said to be as authoritative as the words in the Bible or any other religious scripture?"

How can you know this is real?

"How can I know this is the real Jesus?" Well, you cannot know through the *outer* mind that thinks in words. You can know through your *inner* mind, through what today is called your intuition, your inner knowing. This is what I, 2,000 years ago, called the Key of Knowledge. You might remember that I said: "Woe unto ye lawyers, for you have taken away the Key of Knowledge. Ye entered not in yourselves and those that would enter, ye hindered."

Today, there are also many people who act in this capacity of the lawyers. They have rejected their own inner ability to know reality. They have glorified and deified the outer mind, the intellectual, linear, analytical mind that thinks in words. They have raised up one statement made by words as having some ultimate authority, meaning that all other statements need to be compared to it. If a statement contradicts or goes beyond the authority, then it must be rejected. It cannot be real—so they say!

The lawyers of the modern day – whether they are found in the Christian churches or in the establishments of science and learning – say: "We have the authoritative truth stated in words and anything that contradicts or goes beyond is false."

Well, I have news for you. I am beyond words because *I AM the Word,* the Living Word. You can know that I am real if you are willing to activate the Key of Knowledge, your inner knowing—if you are willing to feel in the center of your chest, in your heart of hearts, the vibration of the words. You will get a stronger impression by hearing the words spoken, but even by reading them in a book, you can tune in to your heart and *know*.

You will know there is a situation in the gospels where two of my disciples met me on the road to Emmaus and they did not recognize my outer form. Afterwards, they realized that while they were with me, their hearts were burning within them.

Well, *is your heart burning within you?* Tune in to that burning, for that burning will tell you the reality of who I am. Then, be willing to look at your outer mind and the arguments that your outer mind is coming up with. Be willing to question: "Is it these arguments that are unreal? Could it be that it is my inner burning, my inner knowing, that is real, and the outer mind cannot show me reality because it can only show me a closed thought system?"

Truly, spirit is beyond any thought system on earth. The real, ascended Jesus Christ is beyond any thought system on earth, any thought system that can be defined with words. *The Word* is more than *words*. The Word is beyond words. No thought system defined with words, not even the Bible, can confine the Word, the Living Word.

This book is for those with open minds

This book is meant to reach out to those who are willing to go beyond words and tune in to the Word. If you are one of them, I congratulate you for having taken the first step towards your ultimate liberation.

When I walked the earth 2,000 years ago, I faced this situation over and over again. I met thousands, even tens of thousands, of people who upon meeting me went through the exact same process that you are going through upon reading this book: "Is this real or is it not? Is it some illusion conjured up by the devil to mislead me?"

All of their fears came up when people met me, just as you might notice your own fears coming up as you read this. Can this possibly be real? Can it possibly be valid? I saw thousands of people take one look at me – or listen to one statement I made that contradicted their mental boxes – and then they rejected me. I could see how they averted their eyes, they turned away, and I knew that they were lost for me at that time. I had to simply move on, for I had only three short years in physical embodiment to fulfill my mission.

Those who did not instantly accept me, I simply had to leave them behind. Those who would not leave their nets, would be caught in those nets for the rest of my mission and ministry. Today, I have more time. Today, it is 2,000 years later, and I am now able to give a message that can liberate greater numbers of people—if they are willing to question their current mental boxes. The irony, of course, is that the mental boxes people need to question in this age have, to a smaller or larger degree, been shaped by the Christian religion.

Jesus' vision for the Christian religion

My vision for the Christian religion was that it would serve as a tool for liberating people from the human mental box. What has happened instead? The Christian religion has been turned into just another human mental box that keeps people trapped.

So many people, over one billion people, are trapped in the Christian mental box, thinking that if they remain in that mental box, they will inevitably be saved. They should read my parable about the wedding feast and how the man who came in without wearing a wedding garment was cast into outer darkness. The wedding garment is a symbol for a state of consciousness, a state of consciousness that is beyond separation.

Separation is anti-christ. Oneness is Christ. The most universal meaning of Christ is that it is the oneness between God and the sons and daughters of God. It is the oneness between the Creator and its creation. Christ was defined by God to ensure oneness between Creator and creation. Christianity was meant to be a movement that gave people a direct inner experience of the Living Spirit, the Living Spirit of Christ, the Word, the Living Spirit of God. Then, they would be able to use that direct inner experience to question and go beyond all of the mental boxes created on earth.

These outer mental boxes are, *all of them,* defined by the mind of anti-christ. This mind has only one goal: to keep you trapped in the state of separation from oneness. It will use anything it can think of to keep you separated from oneness, to keep you trapped in illusion. It will even use the Christian religion, and I can assure you that the Christian religion *has* been used to reinforce the illusion of separation. This I will explain in my coming discourses in this series for those who have ears to hear and eyes to see.

So many people, 2,000 years ago, did not have ears to hear the true, inner, non-verbal message of Christ. They did not have eyes to see the Spirit of Christ. Today, many more people have ears to hear and eyes to see. It is for these people that I offer this and the coming discourses. It is for these people that I offer this Living Word that is the tool you can use to challenge the dead outer word that defines your mental box.

I AM, indeed, the real, living, ascended Jesus Christ. Leave your nets and follow me and I will show you reality, *the reality that I AM.*

2 | HAS CHRISTIANITY TURNED JESUS INTO ANTI-CHRIST?

I AM the Ascended Master Jesus Christ. My aim for this discourse is to show you another aspect of what I think about the religion that claims to represent me on earth. What I wish to discourse on is that Christianity has now become exactly the same kind of religion as the one whose leaders opposed me when I walked the earth in a physical body.

You will recall that it was the leaders of the Jewish religion who plotted to have me condemned to death, even though the sentence was executed by the Roman authorities. This shows you that there has always been a small elite of people who have a desire for ultimate power. One of the ways that they have sought to gain this ultimate power is to set themselves up as the representatives of God on earth.

They define a religion, and then they set themselves up as the leaders of that religion. The people believe that in order to get to God, in order to get salvation, they have to go through the leaders of the earthly religion. This is precisely the kind of power held by the Jewish leaders when I walked the earth. This is precisely what I attempted to challenge when I challenged the scribes and Pharisees, the lawyers and all those who had set themselves up between the people and God.

Jesus challenged the religious elite

What did I say was one of my most important statements? It is that the kingdom of God is within you! Why do you think the leaders of the Jewish religion were so anxious to silence me that they were willing to have me executed in order to shut me up? It was precisely because I said that the kingdom of God is within you. What did *their* religion say? It said that the kingdom of God is *outside of you, far away from you*. There is a gap, a chasm, a distance between you as a human being on earth and the kingdom of God. How can you cross that chasm? Not by your own power, but only by the graces of the leaders of an outer religion on earth.

This was the very belief that allowed them to have near absolute power over the people. They were not about to lose that power so what happened when some wandering preacher started going around their domain and claiming that the kingdom God is within you? They saw that this was the ultimate threat. In the beginning, they ignored me and they laughed, but as I began to gain more and more followers, they became afraid. What if the people listened to this Jeshua, going around, barefoot, and preaching this radical message?

Can you not see that the statement that the kingdom of God is within you is a direct challenge to the power of the members of this elite who have set themselves up between people and God? If the kingdom of God is *within* you, why would you need an *outer* religion and its leaders in order to get to the kingdom? How can you get to the kingdom that is within you by going outside yourself, by going through an institution that is outside yourself?

2 | Has Christianity Turned Jesus into Anti-christ?

The elite that wants absolute power

If you would take an honest look at the history of religion on this earth, you will see that there are two different approaches to religion. The one approach says that in order to be saved, or whatever goal is raised up by that religion, you need to go through some institution or some priesthood outside yourself. The other, the more mystical branch, says that you do not find salvation *outside* yourself; you find it only *inside* yourself.

This is the kind of religion, or approach to religion, that I preached when I walked the earth 2,000 years ago. That is why I was a challenge to the established authorities in Israel, and that is why they had me killed. Is it really that difficult for people in the modern age to see this simple mechanism? How much more clearly could it be expressed?

There is an elite on earth – there always has been, at least in known history – who wants to set itself up and gain ultimate power. One of the most efficient ways to get ultimate power is to get the people to believe that they need the elite in order to get to God's kingdom and avoid a fiery hell with eternal suffering. When people believe in this, then the elite that holds the key to the kingdom has near absolute power over the people.

What did I say, in my last discourse, was my goal of coming to earth? It is to set the people free. One interpretation of this is that I am here to set the people free from the elite, the power elite, that seeks to keep them separated from the kingdom of God.

What did I say about God's desire to give you his kingdom: "Fear not little flock, for it is your Father's *good pleasure* to give you the kingdom." It is not God that makes it difficult for you to enter his kingdom. It is the power elite on earth that wants to make you believe it is difficult to enter God's kingdom. When you believe that you have to go through something outside yourself in order to enter the kingdom, then it is indeed difficult, even impossible, to enter God's kingdom.

In fact, you will never enter God's kingdom as long as you think you have to go through something outside yourself. You will not find the kingdom by observing an outer religion. You will find it only when you go within, look at the beam in your own eye, give up that beam, let your separate sense of identity die and you are spiritually reborn. You are reborn of the spirit into a new person who does not see itself separated from the kingdom.

It is difficult to understand the true message of Christ

It is a change in consciousness that will bring you into God's kingdom because it is a certain state of consciousness that has separated you from that kingdom in the first place. It is absolutely necessary for those who want to know the reality of my true teachings to recognize that there is a power elite on earth who will do everything they can think of, everything they can make people believe, in order to keep you separated from the kingdom of God.

There is an elite, a force of anti-christ, on earth that will do everything it can think of to get you to either not know or to reject the true message of Christ. I will later talk more about this elite and how they perverted the Christian religion, but what I want to talk about here is that it is quite understandable that the Christian religion has been perverted. The reason for this is that it is indeed very difficult for people to grasp the true message of Christ.

May I ask you to consider a thought example? Imagine that you meet a person and you realize in conversation that this person has never tasted an apple. You would then be asked by the person: "Well, what does an apple taste like?" You are now facing a somewhat difficult task of having to describe the taste of an apple with words. When you think about this, you will realize that when you taste something you are having an experience that is beyond words. Describing such a non-verbal experience with words is no easy task, but you do have some recourse because although this person has not tasted an apple, surely, the person has tasted other kinds of fruits and other kinds of food. You can say: "Well, an apple tastes like this," or "An apple tastes like that," and the person will know what you are talking about.

The person has an experience to link to your words, and therefore you might be able to give a description that gives the person a fairly accurate impression of what an apple tastes like. At least, you might be able to give the person enough of an impression that the person develops a desire for the actual experience and therefore goes and buys an apple and takes a bite.

Now, consider a different situation. Consider that you meet a person who has been blind from birth, and you are now asked to describe to that person what an apple *looks* like. You will see that when you were describing the taste, you were comparing the taste of an apple to something that the other person had actually tasted, but this person has never seen anything. How will you describe what an apple looks like to a person who has no visual experience that you can base your description upon? How will that person ever link the words you are saying to an actual experience?

This is the situation I faced when I walked the earth 2,000 years ago. It is the exact same situation I face today as an ascended being. It is the situation faced by all spiritual teachers who are seeking to help humankind escape their current prison.

People have not experienced the Christ mind

I am sent by God to planet earth in order to offer people a morsel of the Christ consciousness. The Christ consciousness is the consciousness of oneness, defined by God to make sure that there is oneness between the Creator and its creation. What has happened to most people on earth is that they have lost their sense of oneness with God. That is why you feel you are outside the kingdom of God.

In reality, God is everywhere, as clearly expressed in the beginning of the Gospel of John: "Without him was not anything made that was made." This refers both to the Christ consciousness in its universal aspect and to the Creator itself. The Creator can create anything it wants, but it must create everything out of its own Being, its own substance, for there is nothing else to create from. This means that God is *everywhere*.

I know that most Christians will immediately say: "Ah, but this is pantheism and this is not the true teaching of Christianity." It may not be the true teaching of Christianity, but *it is the true teaching of Christ*. Without him was not anything made that was made. This was set up by God so that nothing, *no thing,* no form, can be created without the Christ consciousness. This means that the Christ consciousness is embedded within everything, and therefore within everything there is that link to the Creator.

The Christ consciousness is the unifying element

When you look at planet earth, you see many different forms. You may look at a tree, you may look at a mountain or you may look at the sun and the forms are very different. As science has revealed, when you go beyond the outer appearances – when you stop judging after appearances – you see that both the sun and the tree on earth are made from atoms, and *they* are made from even smaller units, called subatomic particles. Beyond even the finest particles discovered by science is an even deeper common element, namely the Word, the Logos, the Christ consciousness.

Without him was not anything made that was made. It is within *everything*. The consequence of this is that right now – when you are sitting on planet earth – you are *not* separated from the kingdom of God. The kingdom of God is the Presence, the consciousness, of God. It is within everything, for without it nothing was made. You can enter the kingdom of God right where you are—right *now*.

Why do you think I walked around Israel saying: "The kingdom of God is at *hand*." What did the preachers of the Jewish religion say? They said: "The kingdom of God is far away and you can enter it in the future. This means that as long as you are here on earth, you are separated from the kingdom of God. You will only enter it in the future if you submit yourself to *our* authority."

I represented the Christ consciousness. I had the ultimate authority of God, but I did not demand that people should submit themselves to my authority as an outer authority. I demanded that they submit to the *inner authority of Christ within themselves.*

I did not come to be elevated to some ultimate or exclusive incarnation of the Christ consciousness. I came to demonstrate that the Christ consciousness is in all people, for without him was not anything made that was made.

The key to entering the kingdom of God is the Christ consciousness. The key to finding the Christ consciousness is to stop looking for it outside yourself and to see that it is right within you. When you discover that inner Christ, *then* you are in the kingdom of God. The difficulty is: How will I – as the representative of the Living Christ, of the Christ consciousness – convey this message to a human being who is trapped in the consciousness of separation and therefore sees itself as being outside the kingdom of God?

You are on earth. You are experiencing life through the perception filter of a particular mental box. Everything you see confirms to you the belief that you are in a world made of separate forms. Surely, the sun looks very different from a tree or a rock, therefore they must be separate forms. What common element could there possibly be? There is no common element when you look at them through the filter, the perception filter, of your physical senses.

Your mind has the ability to go beyond and grasp that there *is* a common element. You may call it subatomic particles, you may call it energy, you may call it the Christ consciousness. How will you grasp this with the outer mind? You cannot, *it is impossible!* You cannot see what you cannot see.

The essential difficulty of a spiritual teacher

Here I am. Whether it was when I walked the earth in a physical body or today, my task is to convey to you the reality of the Christ consciousness. My desire is not to give you a theoretical understanding of the Christ consciousness. My task is to help you *experience* the reality of the Christ consciousness. This is the Key of Knowledge that the lawyers had taken away.

Do you not see that the outer religion and its power elite are based on one particular illusion, the illusion that you are separated from the kingdom of God? I represent the Christ consciousness. I am one with the Christ consciousness and the Christ consciousness *is* oneness. When you are one with the Christ consciousness, you know that all life is one. There is a unifying element behind all outer appearances.

When you have not experienced the Christ consciousness directly, how will you know that what I say is true? I am like the person describing what an apple looks like to a blind person who has no experience to compare to my words. Most people on earth have only experienced separation. They have no experience that I can use to give them an experience of the Christ consciousness.

This is the difficulty that I face as a spiritual teacher. This is why I so often – when I walked the earth 2,000 years ago – talked about those who did not have ears to hear nor eyes to see. This is why it was so difficult for people to grasp the true message that I came to give. This is why I was forced to teach the multitudes in parables. I gave them stories, but what was the aim of those parables? Many people have reasoned that I must have wanted to give people some rules for how to live. This is true, but the real aim of my parables was to challenge people's mental boxes and perception filters. My real hope was that they would gradually snap out of their perception filters and have a direct experience of something beyond the perception filter, the outer mind.

Imagine that you are talking to a blind person and you are getting nowhere with your description of what the apple looks like. Then you realize that the person is not blind in the sense that he cannot see; the person is blind only because he has never opened his eyes. He has never realized that he can open his eyes. When you realize this, you say: "Just open your eyes for a split second!" You know that the person will be blinded if he opens his eyes and keeps them open. But if he could just open them for a split second, he would realize that he *can* actually see, that there is actually something to see, there is an experience beyond the words.

My real goal, when I walked the earth, was to give people even a brief glimpse of the reality of the Christ consciousness and how different it is from their normal experience of life. I did not come to give them words for I knew that words would not convey the fullness of the experience. *I came to give people an experience.*

Experiencing Christ is beyond the outer religion

I am here today to give people an experience for those who are willing, but what does it take to be willing? It takes that you are willing to experience something beyond your normal everyday experience, your normal state of consciousness. What does it take to have that willingness? You cannot be so attached to your normal life experience that you are not willing to go beyond it. This means, among other things, that you cannot be so attached to your outer religion that you are not willing to experience something beyond the doctrines, the worded expressions, of that outer religion.

As I said in my first discourse, the great irony of history is that over a billion people claim to be the followers of Jesus Christ, yet I, as a spiritual, ascended being, have no way of reaching them directly. They are so attached to the form of the outer religion – the words, the rituals, the promises, the world view – that they are not open to a direct experience of the Christ consciousness.

Why is it that, in order to experience the Christ consciousness, you must go beyond your present level of consciousness? It is because the Christ consciousness is beyond any form. It can never be captured by, confined to, a specific form. It is also beyond your current level of consciousness. If you were already in the Christ consciousness, you would be in the kingdom of God and you would experience the kingdom of God. If you are not experiencing the kingdom of God, then how will you ever enter that kingdom? You can do so only by going beyond what separates you from the kingdom—*is that not logical?* What separates you from the kingdom is your present level of consciousness, your present perception filter, that makes it seem like you are not in the kingdom.

Let me explain to you what it truly means that the Christ consciousness is beyond form. Take again the Gospel of John:

"In the beginning was the Word, and the Word was with God because the Word *was* God." Then God started expressing itself as form, but this expression happened through the Christ consciousness, the Word, the Logos. Without the Christ consciousness was not anything made that was made, without the Christ consciousness was not any form made that was made.

This means that if every form is created out of the Christ consciousness, then the Christ consciousness itself must be beyond form. If the Christ consciousness had a specific form, a specific distinguishable form, then it could not be the source of all forms, could it? An apple is different from a pear. You cannot make a pear out of an apple. You can make a pear out of the same substance from which the apple was made by giving that substance a different form. If the substance, the molecules, the atoms, out of which the apple was made could only be expressed as an apple, then you could not use that substance to make a pear. How would you make a pear if atoms could only take the shape of apples? Do you not see, my beloved, this is simple logic. This is childlike logic, but did I not say that unless you become as a little child, you shall not enter the kingdom?

Most people are in the consciousness of death

The situation found on earth 2,000 years ago was that the vast majority of human beings on earth had entered a specific state of consciousness. This is what I today prefer to call the consciousness of separation. When I walked the earth 2,000 years ago, I used a different word. I called it "death," the consciousness of spiritual death. You have lost the awareness that the Christ is in everything, and when you lose the awareness that the Christ is in everything, you are dead in a spiritual sense. You have no life in you for the Christ consciousness is the only source of life. The Christ consciousness is the consciousness of oneness. When you separate yourself from oneness, you die in a spiritual sense. Consider the story in Genesis of how God had told Adam and Eve that they could eat of all of the fruits in the garden, except the one. If they ate of that fruit, they would *surely* die. If you look at the story, you will say that God had apparently lied to Adam and Eve because they ate the fruit and they did not die; they were cast out of Paradise and lived on.

The reality behind the story is that the "fruit of the knowledge of good and evil" represents a specific state of consciousness, namely the consciousness of separation, the consciousness of anti-christ, the consciousness of death. What did the serpent say? "Ye shall not *surely* die. God does not want you to eat the fruit, because he knows that when you eat it, you become as a god, knowing good and evil."

The reality behind the story is that when you partake of the consciousness of separation, the consciousness of anti-christ, you separate yourself from the reality of Christ. What is the reality of Christ? It is that *all* is one because *all* of the forms that you see have sprung from the underlying reality of the Christ consciousness. When you separate yourself from that consciousness of oneness, you are instantly blinded by the illusion that all forms have not sprung from the same source but that they are separate, fundamentally separate.

Once you begin to look at the world through the perception filter of separation, you become subject to the serpentine lie that there are things that are separated from the Christ consciousness. Therefore, *you* can be separated from the kingdom of God. You can be separated from God because God is not in his own creation; God is outside of, far from, his own creation.

Planet earth and the material universe is a sphere separated from God, and that is why it is possible that the devil can rule this world. It is also why it is possible that a power elite can set itself up as the rulers of this world because they stand between you and God. They can appear, not as a devil, but as the saviors of the people who are going to take them into this remote kingdom of God in some remote future time—if only the people will submit themselves to the elite right now, right here on earth, right in this time.

The deception of anti-christ

Do you not see this deception? It is all based on the one claim that something can be separated from the whole, that something can be separated from the Christ consciousness. Once you are separated from the consciousness of oneness, you enter into the consciousness of separation.

In separation there must be not an undivided oneness but a division into at least two separate entities, forms, realities, spheres. The most basic separation created by the consciousness of anti-christ is that there is a world that is separated from God. You are here in this world, God and God's kingdom is somewhere else. This is the basic deception of the consciousness of anti-christ.

I was sent to earth to represent the Christ consciousness. The Christ consciousness is that all is one, and therefore you are not separated from the kingdom of God *in reality*. You are only separated *in your mind;* it is only an illusion that makes you think you are separated. This illusion is created out of the consciousness of anti-christ.

The consciousness of anti-christ is based on you defining two opposite realities. Ponder my words here very carefully and seek for the direct experience that is beyond my words. Surely, I have not come to give you words but an experience. This is what is so difficult for people to grasp.

Christians will immediately say: "But surely, the Christian religion is true and valid. Its world view is correct. It is based on the words of Christ when he walked the earth." Surely, they will say that any viewpoint which contradicts the Christian religion and its doctrines must be false. Therefore, it must be of the devil. Surely, that which is defined by the Christian religion is Christ and anything that contradicts it, is anti-christ.

How Christianity makes Jesus into anti-christ

Most Christians would say that what I am saying here is anti-christ, it is of the devil. Can you not see that this was exactly what the leaders of the Jewish religion said about me when I walked the earth 2,000 years ago? They accused *me* of being of the devil. If they had used the terminology, they would have accused me of being anti-christ. They would have accused me of being *the* anti-christ, as many Christians today will accuse me of being the anti-christ.

The reality is that anti-christ is the mindset that believes it has the capacity and the right to define what is good and what is evil, what is true and what is false, what is Christ and anti-christ. The mindset of anti-christ believes that it can define a form and say: "This form is the exclusive representative of Christ, and therefore anything that is different from or in opposition to it must of necessity be of anti-christ."

The reality of Christ is that no form is the fullness of the Christ consciousness. It is only an expression of it, and therefore if you take an expression of Christ and elevate it to the status of being the full or the exclusive expression of Christ, then you have actually turned that expression of Christ into anti-christ.

This is my problem with the Christian religion. It has turned *me* into anti-christ by elevating me as the exclusive incarnation of Christ. Surely, some will say this is a severe accusation. Is it too severe when it is, in fact, *the truth?*

3 | HOW THE POWER ELITE DESTROYED JESUS' EXAMPLE

I was sent to earth 2,000 years ago to be an expression of the Christ consciousness in a physical body. When you look at the scriptures, you will see that many people failed to recognize me. They simply did not see that there was anything special about me, anything different about me compared to other men. They went about their daily business and completely ignored me even if they had met me in the flesh. You will also see that there were some who did meet me, who did sense there was something special about me, but they felt threatened by that something special. They denied it; they labeled it as being of the devil. After having labeled it, they felt completely justified in first ignoring it and then seeking to silence it and destroy it.

You will also see that there were some who met me and sensed that I had something they did not have. What did I have? I had the Christ consciousness! I was the open door that no human, no human mind, can shut. What was my whole point of taking disciples? It was to share my Spirit, the spirit of the Christ consciousness, with them so that they would not be the blind followers of me as an outer teacher. They would discover that the Christ consciousness they saw in *me* is also in *themselves*.

How to do the works that Jesus did

As *Paul* said: "Let this mind be in you which was also in Christ Jesus." As *I* said: "Those that believe on me, the works that I do shall ye do also and greater works shall ye do." How will you do the works that I did?

You may look at some of the so-called miracles that I performed. You may do, as most people do in the modern age, either deny it or ignore it as being insignificant. Even many Christians – I dare say, a majority of Christians – ignore my miracles. Scientists scoff at these miracles. They believe they have defined a world view that says there are certain laws of nature and nothing can supersede those laws. They are set in stone; they are absolute limitations. The law of gravity makes sure that no one can walk on water. Other laws of nature make sure that when you are dead, you are dead and cannot be raised up. When your arm is withered, it cannot be instantly healed. When the storm is blowing, it cannot be calmed by the command of one person.

What did I say about the works I performed? With men this is impossible, but with God all things are possible. I came to demonstrate that when a human being attains a measure of Christ consciousness – freeing itself from the consciousness of anti-christ, the consciousness of separation – then the power of God can work through that person. It is true that there are laws of nature and that they set limitations, but they set limitations only for people who are trapped in the consciousness of anti-christ, the consciousness of separation.

When you separate yourself from the consciousness of separation and enter into the consciousness of oneness, then the power of God can work through you. The power of God can go beyond the laws of nature anytime it wants to. How will you do the works that I did? Most Christians flat out ignore this statement. Most Christian preachers ignore this statement. How will you do the works that I did? Do you think that I made a false promise when I made that statement? Nay, I made a true promise.

The promise is that if you follow the path I have demonstrated, if you separate yourself from the consciousness of separation and enter into the consciousness of oneness, *then* you can do the works that I did. Or we can say that when you attain the same level of Christ consciousness that I had attained, then the power of God can do the works through *you* that it did through *me*.

Jesus challenged the power of the elite

I came to be an example for all people to follow. I came to demonstrate two things. First, that all people have the potential to attain the Christ consciousness. The Christ consciousness is within all things and therefore the kingdom of God is within *you*. The kingdom of God is not just within *me;* it is within *you*. The kingdom of God was not on earth only when I walked the earth in a physical body 2,000 years ago. The kingdom of God is right *here,* right *now*. The kingdom of God is at hand. It is always at hand for those who have eyes to see and ears to hear, those who are willing to open themselves up to the inner oneness that *is* the kingdom.

The second thing I came to demonstrate is that when you attain the Christ consciousness, you become the open door which no man can shut. You become the open door for the power of God to work through you. Then you can do the works that I did and greater works. In this day and age, it is not necessary to perform the physical miracles. It is necessary to demonstrate a higher state of consciousness and to demonstrate that all can attain it. I came to be an example for the fact that all people have access to the Christ consciousness.

This was in complete opposition to the power elite of the time and the power elite of all times. This was the last thing they wanted preached to the people. Any other message would have been acceptable to them, as long as it maintained the central illusion that you, as a human being on earth, are separated from the kingdom of God, that the kingdom of God is somewhere else far from you and can be attained only at some future time when you are not in physical embodiment. The last thing they wanted was a human being in a physical body demonstrating that he was in the kingdom of God, demonstrating the Christ consciousness. This was absolutely the one message that the power elite did not want to have preached or demonstrated on earth.

What did they do when I dared to be the open door for this message? They instantly killed my physical body, thinking that would silence me. They were thinking that by killing me, they would kill the message, they would kill the Christian movement.

They were very nearly successful, but they had not counted on a simple fact, namely that by killing the body they did not kill my Spirit. As I said: "I will pray the Father that he will send you another Comforter." This comforter became the spirit, the *Holy* Spirit, flowing through my disciples, those who became my true apostles. They realized that they, too, could be the open doors for the spirit that was flowing through me. *That* is how the Christian movement got started: By my disciples going out and demonstrating that they, too, were the open doors for the Living Word and the performing of certain works.

How the power elite perverted Christianity

This did not mean that the power elite was out of options. For the first couple of centuries, they did not really know what to do with the Christian religion. As the Christian religion kept growing, it became obvious to the power elite on this planet that they could not stop this spreading of the Christian religion. What did they, then, do? They decided something very simple: "If we can't beat em, join em. If we cannot stop the Christian religion, let us enter the Christian religion and pervert it from within."

This they did at a fairly early stage. There were people in the Christian movement that wanted to turn it into the classical type of external religion controlled by a small elite. They argued that all these people going around preaching by the spirit were creating chaos, disharmony and disagreement. They argued that the Christian religion ought to have a unified doctrine, a unified set of rituals and a unified organizational structure.

Was this the kind of movement I started? Did I give my disciples a clearly defined written doctrine and say: "Go and preach based on this doctrine?" Nay, I said: "Go and preach by the spirit. Take no thought for what ye shall say because it shall be given onto you through the powers of the spirit when you make yourself an open door."

Did I give them a clearly defined organizational structure set in stone? Nay, I started a movement that was open to the direct guidance of the spirit. It was not *defined* by any power on earth, and therefore it could not be *controlled* by any power elite on earth. It was not defined by any thing on earth and therefore it was open to the flow of the spirit. This *is* the Christ consciousness: the flow of the spirit.

Why was it necessary that I took incarnation on earth? Because people were trapped in the consciousness of separation, the consciousness of anti-christ. They could not see beyond the mental box, the perception filter, created by that consciousness. Their minds had become closed systems, and there was no way for them to reach beyond. It was necessary that someone took embodiment and demonstrated that a human being in a physical body can be the open door for the Christ consciousness, the spirit, flowing through him or her. This was necessary in order to demonstrate the potential that *all people have*.

The mystery of Christ behind all forms

Do you see that the deeper reality is that the Christ consciousness is within everything? The mystery is that some forms can be created and given form based on the consciousness of antichrist, and therefore those forms appear to be separate, to be separate from the Christ consciousness. This is one of the mysteries that makes it difficult to communicate to people the reality of the Christ consciousness. Your outer mind immediately says: "But it cannot be true that all forms have the Christ consciousness within them, for surely, murder, hell or other atrocities cannot be expressions of the Christ consciousness." This is a correct line of reasoning. Many of the conditions you see on earth are *not* expressions of the Christ consciousness, but the mystery that is difficult to grasp with the outer mind is that they still have the Christ consciousness *within* them.

Think about this with a higher form of logic. In the beginning was the Word, and the Word was with God, and the Word *was* God. In the beginning, there was only God, the Creator. There was not yet any manifest form. God could envision innumerable possible forms to create, but a form has to be created out of something; there must be a basic substance. In order to build a house, you must have bricks. You cannot build a house out of thin air for it will not be a structure, it will not be a form. There had to be something that could be shaped into form, and that something is the Christ consciousness.

God is one. The forms envisioned and created by God are all expressions of the oneness of God. God has given self-aware beings free will. This is something I will talk more about in later discourses. For now, I simply want to state the fact that because self-aware beings have free will, they can choose to go away from oneness. When you do separate from oneness, you can create forms that are not expressions of *oneness* but are expressions of *separation*.

In oneness there cannot be two opposites that destroy or cancel out each other. There cannot be good and evil in oneness. There is nothing that opposes oneness. Separation does not oppose oneness. Separation defines two opposites that oppose each other, but those opposites have no reality in oneness. They only have an illusory, temporary reality in the minds of those who have entered separation. Once you enter separation, you think the two opposites are ultimately real. You might even think they were defined by God, but they are not for oneness can never define opposites. Oneness cannot define something in opposition to itself; only separation can define opposites.

What I am saying here is this: All forms have the Christ consciousness within them. Behind the outer appearance is still the Christ consciousness, as both the sun, a tree or a rock is created out of subatomic particles. This does *not* mean that every form is an expression of the Christ consciousness, is an expression of oneness.

Many of the forms and conditions seen on earth are expressions of the consciousness of anti-christ, but the higher logic will show you that something which is created out of anti-christ has no ultimate reality. It is not truly separated from oneness; it has only taken on a temporary, illusory appearance of being separated from oneness. It does not truly exist in some *objective* reality; it exists only in a *subjective* reality created in the mind.

The two kinds of mind

There are two kinds of mind: the mind of Christ and the mind of anti-christ. The mind of Christ is the mind of oneness, and it is the source of life; it has life within it. The mind of anti-christ is the mind of separation; it is the mind of death for it has no life within it. It has no life within it because it contains an internal, inescapable contradiction; two opposites that work against each other and will cancel out and destroy each other.

In the consciousness of anti-christ there is a constant, ongoing struggle between these two opposites. It is this struggle that keeps you separated from the kingdom of God, the kingdom of oneness. The power elite on earth wants to keep you trapped in this struggle because this struggle is the basis for their illusion that you are separated from God and God's kingdom, and that you can only enter God's kingdom by following them.

What did I say was God's promise? It is God's good pleasure to give you his kingdom. God does not require you to struggle in order to attain the kingdom. The only requirement for you attaining the kingdom is that you *stop struggling*.

You can stop struggling only by transcending the consciousness of the struggle, the consciousness of anti-christ. It has defined the two opposites that must be locked in a struggle against each other. It is when you transcend this consciousness that you enter the kingdom of the consciousness of oneness. I came to demonstrate that it is possible for a human being to separate itself from the struggle consciousness. I gave many teachings aimed at helping people do this, one of the most powerful ones was the teaching that you do not resist evil but turn the other cheek.

The true meaning of turning the other cheek

Consider how many people on earth will react if you slap them on one cheek. They will instantly go into a fight-or-flight reaction where they either seek to flee from you or seek to oppose you, possibly even destroy you so you cannot strike them again. Why did I tell people to turn the other cheek? Why did I tell you to stand there and let them hit you again? Because it is the *only* way whereby you can pull yourself away from the consciousness of the struggle. It is the only way whereby you can enter the kingdom of God that is within you and that God is willing to give you without you having to struggle.

Consider again the story of Adam and Eve and the forbidden fruit. In the Garden they had all they needed for their sustenance, and they did not have to struggle for anything. Once they were cast out of paradise, they had to work out their living at the sweat of their brow, meaning that they now had to struggle to obtain everything. The reason they had to struggle was that they had lost the kingdom of God, the consciousness of paradise, the consciousness of oneness. In separation you have to struggle for everything, and as long as you are struggling for something on earth, you will be vulnerable to being controlled by the power elite of anti-christ. How will you enter the kingdom of Christ? How will you truly follow Christ? How will you embrace the true message of Christ? *Only when you stop struggling.*

The consciousness of anti-christ has defined two opposites. It may call them good and evil; it may even say that one of these opposites represents Christ and the other is the devil. This is how the power elite controls you. It makes some people believe that they have to fight what they have labeled as evil. That is why you see people who are willing to kill others in the name of God.

The elite may also say that you should strive to run away from the one opposite and run towards the other, the one they have defined as good. The reality of Christ is that both of the opposites defined through the mind of anti-christ are unreal. None of them will get you to the kingdom.

You will not get to the kingdom of God by destroying *evil*, neither will you get to the kingdom of God by striving for *good*, the relative form of good defined by the mind of anti-christ. You will get to the kingdom only when you stop struggling against evil or struggling to get to good. You need to give up the struggle and accept that it is the Father's good pleasure to give you the kingdom. You do not have to struggle to get what God wants to give you. You have to stop struggling so you can accept that the kingdom of God is already within you.

Destroying Jesus as an example

I came to earth 2,000 years ago to serve as an example that it is possible for a human being in embodiment to attain the Christ consciousness. What did the power elite do when they joined the Christian religion? They attempted to destroy my example so that no one would dare to follow in my footsteps and do the works that I did or even greater works.

This is surely a fundamental problem I have with Christianity: It has turned my true message upside down. It has taken me, who was meant to be an example for all to follow, and elevated me to being an exception. It has said that I, who came as an expression of the Christ consciousness, was the *exclusive* expression of the Christ consciousness. Nay, even more than that, they have said that I was the *only* incarnation of Christ, that I was the fullness of Christ, the fullness of the Christ consciousness.

I was in a physical body on earth. *No* form in the material universe can be the fullness of the Christ consciousness, as I have explained. The Christ consciousness is more than any form, therefore the Christ consciousness has a universal aspect that is more than the person of Jesus Christ who walked the earth. The Christ consciousness is even more than the Ascended Master Jesus Christ. I am not the exclusive expression of the Christ consciousness for my Father's house has many mansions. Those mansions are occupied by many beings who are also expressions of the Christ consciousness. Surely, you do not believe that I am alone up here in heaven, do you?

That would clearly contradict the scriptures of both the Christian and almost any other religion on earth.

Without him was not anything made that was made. *That* includes *you*. You are, in your original, pure form, an expression of the Christ consciousness. You have forgotten your true identity by entering into the consciousness of anti-christ and seeing yourself through that perception filter. Salvation means that you awaken from this illusion and realize who you really are, who you always were. When you accept your true identity, as I accepted *my* true identity, then you too will be the Living Christ in embodiment on earth. This is the true message of Christ that I came to preach and demonstrate 2,000 years ago.

That message was almost completely lost in the scriptures that were written down, for the simple reason that at the time very few people had grasped the reality of that message. Even though the gospel writers were inspired by the spirit, they were not able to grasp the fullness of the message that the spirit wanted to express. Part of that message cannot even be expressed in words; it can only be conveyed through a direct experience.

It was never my intention that my teachings should be confined to four gospels that were elevated to the status of infallibility. That is why I did not write down my teachings. That is why I wanted my early apostles to preach by the spirit and not preach by the book.

Later, those gospels were elevated to the status of infallibility, and it was said that all Christian preachers now had to preach by the book and no longer preach by the spirit. The spirit was lost and thereby the true message of Christ was lost. Of course, nothing is lost forever, for without him was not anything made that was made. At any time, human beings can awaken from the consciousness of separation and embrace the consciousness of oneness.

The potential for an awakening

Even those who are Christians today, even those who have been affected by a Christian doctrine that is clearly out of alignment with the reality of Christ, still have the potential to awaken. Why do you think I bother to give this message? It is because I know that no matter how false of a message you might have received, you still have the potential to awaken instantly, to have the scales fall from your eyes, as happened to Paul on the road to Damascus.

That potential can never be lost, precisely because the Christ consciousness is within every form. Surely, some of the current Christian doctrines are out of alignment with the reality of Christ. They are not expressions of Christ, but nevertheless the Christ consciousness is behind the outer form. If you are willing to look beyond the outer form, you can awaken to the reality of Christ. You can have the scales fall from your eyes in a blinding flash, and you can encounter my Spirit, my Living Spirit, as Paul encountered it on the road to Damascus.

The question is not whether you *can* encounter my Living Spirit; the question is only whether you *are willing* to encounter that spirit. For most people this means that they must be willing to question the doctrines that they have been brought up to see as being infallible and therefore beyond questioning.

I have given this book for those who are willing to question the outer doctrines and to keep doing so until they have opened their minds sufficiently that they can encounter my Living Spirit. I am not here to give you teachings; I am here to give you teachings that will open your mind to the point where you can experience something beyond the words. You can experience the Spirit that I AM for I AM the Spirit of the real, living, ascended Jesus Christ.

4 | PETER REPRESENTED THE SATANIC CONSCIOUSNESS

In this discourse I wish to speak about my disciple, Peter, and the consciousness that he represents. Surely, this consciousness became the foundation for the Roman Catholic Church, and as such it has, to a large extent, formed the foundation for all of the Christianity that followed after, at least in the Western world.

First, I wish to speak about the fact that when I walked the earth 2,000 years ago, the greatest challenge I faced was those who were in the literal, linear mindset. You have always had – if you look back over the history of this earth – two approaches to religion or spirituality. One is the linear, literal approach where you take everything that is said from a higher realm and you want to interpret it with the outer mind, with the intellect that thinks in linear, literal terms. You want to believe that a scripture given by a higher authority should be interpreted to mean what the outer mind thinks it means.

The consciousness that opposes Christ

In contrast to this approach, you see the inner, mystical approach where people realize that an outer scripture, given in words, is meant simply to attune your mind to a reality, to a spirit, beyond the words. Obviously, there were those in the Jewish religion 2,000 years ago who took the outer approach, the linear approach, and these where the ones who rejected me.

What did they do? They took the existing scriptures from the Torah and they used them to argue against me. They attempted to find some point where I contradicted or went beyond the old law, and then they used this to say that I could not possibly be a true prophet or even the Messiah.

This is the state of consciousness that opposed me 2,000 years ago, and it opposes the Living Christ today. Today, one of the main focuses for this state of consciousness is precisely the religion that calls itself Christianity and that claims to represent me on earth. Where are the scribes and the Pharisees today? Many of them are in the Christian religion. Many of them are sitting in their churches, feeling holier than thou, feeling that they have the only true interpretation of the scriptures and that by interpreting the scriptures in a linear fashion or according to their doctrines, they have captured the fullness and the essence of Christ.

I can tell you that if you think I am happy with the fact that the religion that claims to represent me on earth has been taken over by the very mindset that opposed me when I walked the earth, then you are severely mistaken. I am not happy with this fact whatsoever, although I am not entirely surprised. This state of consciousness has always been around, and it believes it is right. It has an aggressive intent of propagating itself by either getting people to accept it or by subduing those who will not.

What did this consciousness do to me when I walked the earth in a physical body? It killed me in order to destroy what it saw as a threat to its existence and its hold over the people. I came to set the people free. How do you set people free? Why do you need to set them free? Because they are trapped in a lower state of consciousness. How do I set them free from a limited state of consciousness? I can do so only by challenging that state of consciousness, including the religious scriptures that were used to build that mental box.

The very consciousness I am talking about will not allow me to challenge the mental box. It will say that if I do challenge the mental box, I cannot be a true prophet, a true Messiah or a true spiritual teacher. These are the people who do not have ears to hear nor eyes to see when they meet the Living Christ in the flesh or when they meet a representative of the Living Christ. They simply do not recognize that the Living Christ is beyond their own mental box. They are so emotionally attached to their mental box that they will not allow the Living Christ to offer them an alternative that could set them free from their self-created prison.

This is the essence of what I meant when I talked about the lawyers who had taken away the Key of Knowledge. The Key of Knowledge is the Christ consciousness. The Key of Knowledge only works for you if you are willing to let the Christ consciousness challenge your mental box and take you, your spirit, beyond the box. *This,* the scribes and Pharisees were not willing to do. Today, the scribes and Pharisees of the Christian religion are no more willing to do this than those who were the leaders of the Jewish religion 2,000 years ago. The scribes and Pharisees of today reject the Living Christ as the scribes and Pharisees of old did back then.

The Alpha and the Omega of evil

Is there anything new under the sun? Indeed, there is *something* new for in this age many more people do have ears to hear the

Christ that is beyond the common mental box. For those who have ears to hear, let me show you how this very consciousness has influenced the Christian religion. There are many people who are aware that there was a being who personified evil, or the opposition to God, who is named Lucifer. There are also many who are aware that there is another dark being named Satan.

We might say that Lucifer represents the Alpha and Satan represents the Omega. Lucifer represents a state of consciousness that wants to shut God out from this world. As I have said, the Creator is beyond its creation, the formless God does not express itself directly in this world. Shutting God out of this world is, in one sense, not difficult. God respects the free will of the people in the material realm. God expresses itself through those who are in embodiment. This is the whole point of the incarnation of the Living Christ.

What Lucifer wants to do is to shut out the Living Christ from this world. Lucifer represents the consciousness that does not want the Living Christ to take embodiment. There are many people on earth who are trapped in the Luciferian consciousness. They do not have eyes to see nor ears to hear when the Living Christ appears, not necessarily in the form of a human being but also in the form of a spiritual teaching, even a teaching that is not openly spiritual but nevertheless challenges some mental box, some mental prison.

What I want to discourse on here is the Omega aspect of this, which is the consciousness represented by Satan. You will know, if you have studied the scriptures, that there is a passage in the Gospel of Mathew that records how I once asked my disciples what people were saying about me. They told me various things the people were saying, and then I asked them what *they* were saying about me. Peter says that I am the Living Christ, the son of God. I then said to Peter that this is the rock upon which I will build my church. This is the quote that has been taken by many Christian ministers and leaders as a validation for the Christian religion in its current form.

It has certainly been taken by the leaders of the Roman Catholic Church as the justification for saying that this church carries on the tradition of Peter and is based on the authority of Peter. This church and its leaders have elevated Peter to the status of being my primary disciple, my first apostle and the first Pope of the church I intended to start.

What I have just told you is that there is a consciousness represented by Lucifer that wants to shut out Christ from this world. When people are blinded by this state of consciousness, they cannot even recognize the Living Christ. They cannot recognize anything that comes from outside their own mental box, or at least they cannot recognize it as having something to offer them.

They are so identified with their mental box that they do not want their mental box challenged. They see no need to be free of their mental box, and therefore they feel threatened by anything that comes to free them. They reject the very savior sent by God to set them free. This is the consciousness of Lucifer, and it prevents people from even recognizing the Living Christ as having anything special to offer.

Why Jesus called Peter Satan

If you take the quote I referred to above, you will see that Peter was not blinded by this state of consciousness. On reflection, this should be no surprise. How could anyone blinded by the consciousness of Lucifer become one of my disciples? It should therefore be possible for today's Christians – at least those who are open-minded – to see that when I said that this is the rock upon which I will build my church, I was not simply referring to one particular historical person. I was referring to the ability to recognize the Living Christ and recognize that the Living Christ has something to offer you that is beyond your current mental box. Peter had recognized me and had been willing to follow me as one of my disciples. So had, of course, my other disciples. If you look honestly at the disciples, you will see that they were all somewhat different. They all had their various backgrounds, their reasons for following me, but they were following me because they recognized that I had something out of the ordinary, something that they needed and wanted. This means that none of my disciples were blinded by or identified with the consciousness represented by Lucifer.

If you have read the Gospel of Matthew carefully, you will know that after the quote where I say that this is the rock upon which I will build my church, there is another passage. I start telling my disciples what will happen to me and how I will be persecuted. What I am basically telling them between the lines is that I will be persecuted by the consciousness of Lucifer, that I will be humiliated and put down by this consciousness. Peter then gets upset with me—and by the way, Peter often got upset with me and with my teaching. In the instance recorded in the scriptures, Peter starts arguing with me, disciplining me, telling me that these things that I am prophesying shall not come to pass because they are beneath me.

If you have read the passage, you will know my reaction. What did I say to Peter: "Get thee behind me, Satan: thou art an offense to me: for thou savourest not the things that be of God, but those that be of men." If you read these two passages together, you must ask yourself how I can, at one moment, say that Peter is the rock upon which I will build my church and then the next moment denounce him as Satan.

I have now given you the foundation for understanding this mystery. When I said that this is the rock upon which I will build my church, I was referring to a specific state of consciousness, the consciousness that makes you able to recognize the Living Christ. When I later denounced Peter as Satan, I was again not referring to a particular historical person. I was denouncing a state of consciousness that is represented by Satan. This is the state of consciousness which recognizes that the Living Christ has a right to express itself in this world, but it wants the Living Christ to express itself in a way that *conforms to* certain conditions defined in this world.

Be careful to use your heart to go beyond the linear mind when you ponder this teaching. It is a key to understanding what is lacking in the Christian movement and what could transform it into the movement I envisioned it to be.

Many Christians do not recognize Christ

The Living Christ comes into this world to set the captives free. This does not mean that he physically leads them out of the land of Egypt into the promised land of Israel. Egypt was a symbol for a state of consciousness.

It is actually a symbol for a state of consciousness in which the people are dominated by Pharaoh, which represents the Luciferian consciousness. Moses is a symbol for a leader who can lead the people beyond the Luciferian consciousness. That is why he had to physically lead them for they needed a leader who could do something for them physically. That is why – when Moses ascended the mountain and received the first commandments from God – the people in his absence had created a golden calf. They were still in such a low consciousness that they were not able to grasp the formlessness of spirit. They needed something concrete, physical, linear to worship

When I appeared later, I represented a higher level of consciousness. I came to set the people free, not by physically leading them from one location to another, but by leading them in consciousness, by leading them beyond both the Luciferian and the Satanic consciousness, both the perversion of the Alpha and the perversion of the Omega.

Only those who had already started to go beyond the Luciferian consciousness could recognize me and become one of my disciples and one of my early followers. Today, only those who have started to go beyond the Luciferian consciousness can truly recognize Christ. In this, I do not count all Christians for the Christian religion has become an outer thing and many people have been born and brought up in the Christian religion. They have never truly grasped what the Living Christ is. They were only taking over a religion and a culture that was given to them.

My early disciples and followers, you will recognize, were not brought up in a Christian religion. There *was* no Christian religion. There was no outer church with doctrines, scriptures, rituals, elaborate cathedrals and churches on every street corner. Those who were my early followers had to recognize me and recognize that I had something to offer, and it is the same today. Many call themselves Christians but have not had the inner realization that I offer something more than the normal human state of consciousness.

Exposing the consciousness of Satan

The first step towards liberation is that you recognize that you are trapped in a limited state of consciousness. You recognize that you have a true inner desire to be free of that state of consciousness. Then you recognize that you cannot free yourself, you cannot pull yourself up by your own bootstraps.

If you are to be free of your state of consciousness, you need something from beyond your mental box. You need something from a higher realm that comes in and offers you the rock of Christ. The rock of Christ is a symbol for a state of consciousness that is beyond anything on earth, beyond any mental box created in the material world. The rock of Christ is incorruptible because the consciousness of Lucifer cannot shut it out and cannot change it. The consciousness of the material world has no influence on the rock of Christ and that is why the consciousness of Christ, the Living Christ, is the only way for you to raise yourself above the consciousness of this world and escape the clutches of the prince of this world.

You must have something from outside your current state of consciousness. Otherwise, your state of consciousness will remain a closed system that you cannot break out of. You are simply walking around in circles. Your consciousness has become a closed loop from which there is no escape. You are, so to speak, treading water and there is no way for you – when you are in the water – to raise yourself above the water, at least not by your own power. You can raise yourself above the water only if someone throws you a rope so you have something from beyond the water to hold on to and then raise yourself up by pulling your body above the water.

This is the same with the mind. You need something from outside the material state of consciousness that you can use to pull yourself above it, and that something is the Christ consciousness. After you have recognized that you are in a limited state of consciousness – after you have recognized the Living Christ offering you an alternative – now comes the most critical phase.

You see, 2000 years ago, there were quite a number of people on planet earth who had started to go beyond the Luciferian consciousness, but there were very few people who had started to go beyond the Satanic consciousness. This is what was represented by Peter.

He was a representative of the stage where you have started to go beyond the Luciferian consciousness and therefore you can recognize the Living Christ. You are willing to follow the Living Christ, but you have not started to go beyond the Satanic consciousness. There is a limit to how far you are willing to follow the Living Christ. You think that after you have recognized the Living Christ and done something physical to follow him, you should be home free, *he* should do the rest. You have in your mind certain limitations for how far you think you need to go. There is a limit to how much you think that you personally have to change yourself. There is a limit to how much of your mental box you need to throw away in order to be a follower of Christ. This also means that there is a limit to how much you are willing to allow the Living Christ to challenge your mental box, your preconceived opinions and expectations of what it means to be a disciple of Christ.

You have in your mind defined certain conditions for what you think it means to be a spiritual or religious person, a follower of Christ or of any other religion. You want the Living Christ to validate these conditions rather than challenge them. You do not want the Living Christ to take you beyond them. You want the Living Christ to validate the belief upon which they rest, namely that by living up to conditions in the material universe, you can qualify for entry into the spiritual realm. This is the consciousness of Satan.

If you are identified with this consciousness, I cannot help you. That is why my only option is to say: "Get thee behind me, Satan!" You are – or rather the consciousness is – an offense to me. I cannot help you by validating or conforming to the very state of consciousness that keeps you outside the kingdom of heaven. *Will you please listen to this statement!*

I am the Living Christ and I am here to set you free. What I have to set you free from is a state of consciousness. In order to set you free from that state of consciousness, I must challenge it and give you the tools to go beyond that state of consciousness. If you want me to conform to and validate your current state of consciousness, *I cannot free you.* You do not have eyes to see nor ears to hear.

Peter repeatedly rejected Christ

If you will study the scriptures again, you will see that there are other examples in the scriptures where Peter illustrated this very state of consciousness. Take the situation where I am put on trial and Peter denies me three times. Why did Peter deny me, why did he deny that he was one of my disciples? Because he had certain conditions in his mind that prevented him from going all the way with me. If Peter had truly believed that I was the Messiah, why would he not have been willing to be crucified with me? How could this in any way have been a detriment to Peter? Surely, he would have been resurrected with me.

There were certain conditions, defined in this world, that Peter was not willing to let go of in order to follow me. What do you think I really meant when I said that unless you are willing to lose your life for my sake, you cannot be one of my true followers and you cannot find the eternal life that comes after the resurrection and through the ascension? I did not mean that you have to lose your physical life in order to be a true follower of Christ. I meant you have to be willing to lose the state of consciousness that is defined in this world and that defines you as a being who is dependent upon conditions in this world.

The Living Christ is completely independent of any conditions in this world. That is why he can serve as the savior who can pull the people beyond their conditional state of consciousness. In order to truly follow Christ, you have to give up *all* of the conditions defined in this world. They are all defined either by the consciousness of Lucifer or the consciousness of Satan. *There are no exceptions to this!*

Unless you are willing to lose your mortal, material sense of life, you cannot follow me all the way into the kingdom of God. Peter three times refused to openly declare his oneness with me before men. What did I say: "He who denies me before men, him must I deny before the Father." It truly means that if you are not willing to become one with the Living Christ – to become one with the Christ consciousness, to let this mind be in you which was also in Christ Jesus – then you cannot enter the kingdom of heaven.

The *only* way to enter the kingdom of heaven is that you personally attain the Christ consciousness by overcoming, by raising yourself above, the consciousness of this world, the prince of this world. You must come to the state where the prince of this world comes and has nothing in you because you have been willing to look at the beam in your own eye and remove all elements of both the Luciferian and the Satanic state of consciousness. You have been willing to challenge the elements that make up these mental boxes. You have systematically let go of these illusions that pull your mind in different directions so that you are a house divided against itself that cannot stand. Instead, you have been willing to let your eye be single, the undivided vision of the Christ mind, so you can rightly divide the word of truth. This is how you free yourself from the consciousness of this world and this is how you are a true follower of Christ.

As long as you have conditions for how far you are willing to go and what you are willing to give up in order to follow the Living Christ, then you are not a true follower of Christ. You cannot walk with me all the way to the Christ consciousness. You will see a state of separation between yourself and the Christ consciousness. You will think you are not worthy to be the Christ in embodiment, and this is precisely what Peter did not think.

He had seen me declare my worthiness. I know that most Christians today are looking back at this through the Christian perception filter, which I will shortly expose as the fallacy that it is. I know that you think I was fundamentally different from Peter, and therefore it was perfectly right that he could not see himself as being one with me or as being at the same level as me. Peter was not at the same level as me because he did not have the spiritual attainment that I had. But Peter still had the potential to put on the Christ consciousness, and he was meant – if he had lived up to his highest potential – to affirm this potential and demonstrate it.

Not all who put on the Christ consciousness have the same long-term spiritual attainment, but all who are true followers of Christ recognize that the goal of following Christ is to put on the Christ consciousness. You put on the Christ consciousness by realizing that you are *worthy* to put on the Christ consciousness because *God created you worthy*. The entire illusion perpetrated by both the consciousness of Lucifer and the consciousness of Satan is that because you are in this world, there is something fundamentally flawed with you. This flaw makes you unacceptable to God so that he will not let you into his kingdom.

5 | THE SATANIC FOUNDATION OF THE CATHOLIC CHURCH

You have grown up in a Christian tradition that is based on the idea of original sin, the claim that you were somehow created or born in sin. In reality, your lifestream, as a spiritual, formless being, was not created in sin; it was created in God's perfection. You have forgotten who you are, you have forgotten your potential. I am come as the Living Christ to awaken you to your true identity as a son or daughter of God and to your true potential to reclaim that identity and to take dominion over the earth through the Christ consciousness.

You take dominion by you accepting your Christ potential and then putting on the Christ consciousness. This was the highest potential for Peter, as it was for all of my disciples. Peter was not willing to go all the way to this stage. He had conditions, opinions, expectations that he was not willing to give up. Peter therefore came to embody the Satanic consciousness, which wants you to believe that there will forever be a gap between you and Christ, between you and the kingdom of God. It wants you to believe that you cannot cross that gap on your own. You need an outside savior to come in and take you across the chasm.

Why did I say that the kingdom of God is within you if you need an outside savior? Do you not think that I, as the Living Christ, knew what it takes to be saved? Certainly, I knew, and that is why I told you the truth that the kingdom of God is within.

What Christ can and cannot do for you

Take note of the subtlety that the consciousness of Satan wants you to overlook. I have just said that when you are trapped in the consciousness of Satan, you need something from outside that consciousness, outside your mental box, in order to pull yourself beyond the mental box. That something is the Christ. The Christ consciousness is the savior, but it is not the savior in the sense that it physically takes you into the kingdom, nor is it the savior in the sense that it changes your mind.

You have been given free will by God. *Your* state of mind is *your* responsibility. Your free will is still *free*. Whatever choices you have made in the past have not taken away your ability to make choices in the present. This means that any choice you have made in the past, you can undo by making a different choice in the present. This is the reality of what God has created.

The Satanic consciousness wants you to not know this or even to deny this. It wants you to believe that because of something that happened in your past – whether it was your own choices or the choice made by Adam and Eve – you are now damaged goods, and you cannot return to God's kingdom on your own power.

The Christ cannot take you into the kingdom. The Christ can give you the rock of Christ, a lifeline, so that you can pull yourself into the kingdom by pulling yourself beyond the consciousness of duality and separation, the consciousness of mortality. This is what the Christ *can* do for you, but *you* must, as I illustrated in my parable, multiply the talents instead of burying them in the ground.

The Christ comes to you and gives you a morsel of truth. You are meant to take that into your being and allow it to become like the leaven that raises the whole loaf of your consciousness. When you do this, you have multiplied the talents, especially when you also dare to express it in helping others raise their consciousness.

When you multiply the talents, you will be given more. When you internalize and multiply *that,* you will be given even more. This is how the Christ gradually raises your consciousness until you come to the point where you can consciously acknowledge and accept that you are in the kingdom of God. This is not because you have entered the kingdom of God but because you have shifted your consciousness to the point of realizing that you *always were* in the kingdom of God.

The Catholic Church as a political institution

What you realize when you put on the Christ consciousness is that nothing is separated from God. This is the Luciferian and the Satanic illusions combined. You realize that these are illusions, and therefore you always were in the kingdom. Now that you are accepting that you are in the kingdom, you have become the open door which no man, meaning no force in this world, can shut.

Look at Peter. He first denied me when I was there during my trial. Later, when he comes to Rome, even though he does preach the message of Christ and is arrested by the Roman authorities, he demands that he be crucified upside down because even at this point he denies that he is worthy to be the Christ. He denies his worthiness to follow me all the way into oneness with me, oneness with my individual Christ consciousness and with the universal Christ consciousness. This is the legacy, this is the very state of consciousness, that became the foundation for the Roman Catholic Church. Note that I say *Roman* Catholic Church.

If you know anything about history, you should know that Christianity only became a major religious force when the Roman Emperor Constantine made it the state religion of the Roman Empire. From its very inception, the Roman Catholic Church was not the kind of church that I had envisioned. Constantine had not been converted; he had not seen the reality of Christ. Constantine was still blinded by the Luciferian consciousness. Peter had at least recognized me, Constantine never did. He made a political decision that rather than fighting Christianity, he would seek to use it to unify his empire. He thought that he could turn Christianity into the kind of religion that would give him full control over the empire that was threatening to fracture.

Do you see what this truly means? Constantine was trapped in both the Luciferian and the Satanic consciousness. He simply wanted a religion that could be used to control the people. This is also what the leaders of the Jewish religion wanted when I walked the earth. That is why they would not allow me to challenge their control over the people and why they silenced me, or attempted to.

Constantine had no vision whatsoever of what the Living Christ means. Neither did those who became the leaders of this new Roman state religion. They thought that by overcoming the persecution and by Christianity becoming the recognized state religion, they would attract more converts to the outer religion. They thought this was doing the work of Christ, and therefore they were willing to compromise the teachings of Christ in order to attract more followers to an outer organization.

They had now become focused on the outer religion of Christianity rather than the inner teachings of Christ. You might recall that I just said that this is exactly what the consciousness represented by Peter does. It defines a set of conditions on earth, and then it wants the Living Christ to adapt to them, to conform to them and to validate them.

The Catholic Church is blinded by Satan

The leaders of the Roman Catholic Church believed that they had the right to define the Nicene creed and a set of doctrines that were clearly – for anyone who has eyes to see – out of alignment with the inner teachings of Christ. The Roman Catholic Church was *never* the kind of church that I envisioned when I said: "This is the rock upon which I will build my church."

Yes, you *can* say that the Roman Catholic Church represents the consciousness of Peter, and it is based on the ability to recognize that Christ has something to offer. It is not completely blinded by the consciousness of Lucifer. Yet it is *completely* blinded by the consciousness of Satan. The Roman Catholic Church, from its very inception, believed that it was able to define an outer institution and an outer doctrine that accurately and fully represented Christ.

What have I said was the entire purpose for the coming of Christ? It is to take you beyond any mental box created on earth. How can an institution defined on earth be said to be an accurate and complete representation of Christ? I never – *ever* – meant for any organization to claim that it was the exclusive representative of Christ on earth.

This is something you cannot understand when you are blinded by the consciousness of Satan, but those who have begun to look beyond this consciousness can indeed grasp it. I said earlier that 2,000 years ago some people had begun to look beyond the consciousness of Lucifer, and that is why I was able to come to this planet, but many had not begun to look beyond the consciousness of Satan. Today, this has changed. Many more people are willing and able to start looking beyond the consciousness of Satan and that is why I am giving this teaching and other teachings.

The fundamental question for all Christians

Many of these people are no longer found in Christian circles. Many of these people have grown up in a Christian culture and because they were able to see beyond the consciousness of Satan, they could see the hollowness or the fallacy of Christian culture, beliefs and doctrines. They could see the shocking difference between the words of Christ and the outer behavior of the Christian churches throughout the ages. Consider how the Roman Catholic Church – that claims to be the only true church of Christ on earth – precipitated so many things that clearly cannot be in accordance with the teachings of Christ, even the rudimentary teachings recorded in the scriptures.

If you are willing to take an objective look at history, you can see that the Roman Catholic Church eradicated the knowledge of the Greek philosophers. How could this be in accordance with my teachings? Did I not say: "Ask and you shall receive, seek and you shall find?" How is destroying knowledge in accordance with the words of Christ? You will see that there were many schisms in the early church and that they always ended with those who had power silencing or expelling the opposition. How could this be in accordance with the teachings of Christ?

The Catholic Church precipitated the inquisition, the crusades, the witch-hunts, the persecution of scientists. Even by the lowest estimates, millions of people were killed and tortured. How could this be in accordance with the teachings of Christ to not resist evil, to turn the other cheek, to do unto others as you would want them to do unto you, to love God with all your heart, mind and soul and to love you neighbor as yourself? If you cannot see that the teachings I gave 2,000 years ago were completely nonviolent, then you are blinded by the consciousness of Satan.

The inescapable question that all who call themselves Christians should be asking is this: "How is it possible that a religious institution, which claims to be based on the non-violent teachings of Christ, could ever precipitate and justify violence?" This is a simple, fundamental question that *all* Christians should be considering. Then they should be willing to see that there is only one possible answer.

The answer is that this institution, which claims to represent Christ, has become influenced and controlled by the very consciousness of anti-christ, the consciousness of Satan. *There is no other possible explanation!*

Killing in the name of Christ is Satanic

It does not matter whether the Christian religion killed one million people or one single person. The very proof of the problem is that the Christian religion has been willing to use the teachings of Christ to justify violence. Consider a Catholic inquisitor during the Middle Ages. He spends his day in a medieval torture chamber, precipitating the most horrendous torture on people who are his own countrymen and even in some cases Christians.

He tortures them in a most brutal way in order to get them to renounce what he believes is the doctrine of Satan. Then, after a day's work, he goes into his Catholic church, kneels before the statue of the crucified and bleeding Christ, looks up at this statue and he thinks I am looking back at him with approval of what he has done in my name.

What makes it possible for a human being to so pervert a nonviolent teaching into a justification for violence? It is precisely the consciousness of Satan that makes it possible for human beings to recognize the Living Christ, but then to take the teachings and the example of the Living Christ and force it into a mental box constructed from the consciousness of anti-christ. Once this has happened, people believe that Christ has now validated the very conditions defined by the consciousness of anti-christ.

Satan and Lutheran churches

This is what is represented by the consciousness of Peter. This is what became the very foundation for the Roman Catholic Church. This consciousness is still woven into the fabric of this church. I know many Christians will say: "But we are Lutherans."

Luther, despite his good intentions, was not able to carry through the reform that was needed. He was able to take some elements out of the Christian religion that had been added by the Roman Catholic church, but he was not able to put back in what had been taken out. This was partly because he had no written record of it, not knowing which scriptures had been banned as heresy, and partly because he was not able to free himself sufficiently from the consciousness of Satan.

He saw the fallacy of some of the conditions defined by the Catholic leaders, but he defined other conditions and they also sprang from the consciousness of Satan. Therefore, Lutheran Christianity today is also based on, influenced by, the consciousness of Satan. It has the conditions springing from the consciousness of Satan woven into the very fabric of its organization, its doctrines, its culture, its world view.

Do you think that I, the ascended Jesus Christ, am happy with this state of affairs? Well, if I was, I would not be dictating this book, would I? I am dictating this book because I know that enough people, both inside and outside of the Christian religion, now have eyes to see and ears to hear the reality of Christ that is beyond the consciousness of Satan.

Jesus wants Christianity reformed

It remains to be seen whether there are enough people who are willing to heed these words and therefore reform the Christian religion and bring it back towards the kind of organization that it could be. It remains to be seen whether there are enough people who will take these outer words and use them as a stepping stone to make their own personal contact with me in their hearts so that I can give them direct inner guidance for how to reform the Christian religion.

Do I want to see the Christian religion reformed? Yes, if it can be done based on a willingness to recognize the consciousness of Christ and recognize that it is completely beyond the conditions defined by the Satanic consciousness. If this willingness is not there, then I would rather see the Christian religion shrink into obsolescence, as it is in the process of doing. I will not allow my light to reinforce a religion that has so outlived its time and its purpose.

There was a time when it was allowed for the Christian religion to be in the state it was in because there was not a critical mass of people who had started raising themselves above the consciousness of Satan. The outer religion simply outpictured the consciousness of the people. Why do you think that in the old part of the Christian world people have been leaving Christianity in droves? It is because they have started to awaken within, even though they do not understand with their outer minds why they have become dissatisfied with the Christian religion.

By dictating this book and bringing these words into the physical, I am creating a physical focal point of what is going on in the consciousness of the people. This will be a turning point, as it was a turning point when I took physical embodiment 2,000 years ago.

In this day and age, I do not need to take physical embodiment, but I do need a physical focal point for bringing the shift in consciousness down into the physical, material spectrum. This I have done and will continue to do in this book. It remains to be seen how people will use their free will to take this material and run with it.

Will they shrink away from it by clinging to the consciousness of Peter? Will they use the consciousness of Satan to denounce this material, to deny it, or to explain away with clever reasoning why they do not have to follow it or act upon it? Or will they, as Paul on the road to Damascus, allow me to take the scales from their eyes so that they may see, in a blinding light, the true light of Christ that I am in this day and age.

Two thousand years ago I said: "I have yet many things to say unto you but you cannot bear them now." People could not bear them because they were not ready to see beyond the consciousness of Satan. Today, many more people can bear them and so here is the physical, undeniable word of the Living Christ.

Do with me as thou wilt, just as people did 2,000 years ago. Whatever you do, I shall look to my Father and say: "Father, forgive them, for they know not what they do." I know that there are a few people who will denounce and deny me and they *know* what they are doing. To these I say: "Father, forgive them, even though they know what they are doing." *I am the living, ascended Jesus Christ.*

6 | THE INNER MEANING OF THE FALL OF MAN

Now that I have given you a somewhat stern discourse on the Peter consciousness and how it has affected Christianity, let me give you a somewhat softer evaluation of why and how this happened. When you look at it realistically, from a higher perspective, you see that what actually determines the evolution or growth of humankind is the level of the collective consciousness. The psychologist Carl Jung was the first to speak about a collective unconscious that he saw as a mind that was shared by all people on earth.

Such a collective consciousness is indeed a reality, which you have better foundations for understanding today than my disciples and followers had 2,000 years ago. Today, you know the scientific reality that everything is made from energy. This means that everything has a certain energy component. It therefore becomes possible to envision that the human body is connected to the mind because the mind is an energy field. If you take the logical consequence of the teachings of Albert Einstein, you will see that even the physical body is an energy field and that is why the body and the mind are connected.

If you take this to the scale of the earth itself, you see that even what you call the physical earth is actually a vibrating energy field. It seems solid and unchanging to the physical senses, but that is because your physical senses are calibrated to detect vibrations within a certain range, within a certain spectrum. That is why your senses cannot see that what seems like solid matter is actually made from vibrating energy.

When you realize that the earth truly is an energy field, it becomes possible to accept that there is an energy field beyond or around the physical planet. This energy field is not separated from the physical planet. In fact, the physical planet is the most dense aspect of this total field. When you realize that such an energy field exists, you also realize that it can act as a unifying component that ties together all people on earth. Because the physical planet is inside the larger energy field, all human beings are inside this field.

What drives humanity's progress?

Your individual mind is inside the larger energy field of the earth, and therefore your individual mind is inside the larger collective mind. Why has there been a progression in outer technological development over the past several thousand, and especially the past several hundred, years? It is because there has been a raising in the vibration of the energies of the collective energy field. When you have this perspective, you see that human history can be understood in terms of the energy field or the collective consciousness.

I am not here saying that the collective energy field can be understood in completely mechanical terms, as it is currently envisioned by many scientists. I am not here giving a materialistic view of the energy field. I am a spiritual being, and I know the reality that there is something beyond the material realm. The collective energy field is not simply a mechanical field, it is

6 | The Inner Meaning of the Fall of Man

very much connected to or has a conscious component. That is why I talk about a collective *consciousness*.

We can therefore say that human history can be understood in terms of the level of the collective consciousness. This becomes important when you compare it to some of the teachings found in the Bible. You will see, for example, that Genesis says that there was a time in the past where Adam and Eve lived in a so-called paradise. I have talked about the tendency to take everything literally and interpret it with the linear mind. You will never understand the subtler more mystical aspects of the Bible if you attempt to take everything literally. It is far more productive to interpret everything in the Bible as a symbol for something, as I said that Peter is a symbol for a certain state of consciousness.

The fall into a lower state of consciousness

The story of the Garden of Eden is a symbol for what has happened to humankind's collective consciousness. Adam and Eve were not the only people in the garden. There was never a point where there were only two people on earth. This is a wrongful, linear and literal interpretation of the Bible. Genesis gives an account of what happened to all people on earth at a time in the past. It is meant to be symbolic, and Adam and Eve should be seen as examples, representatives or archetypes of what has happened to all human beings.

Indeed, there was a time in the distant past – and I am not giving you a figure because I do not want you to activate the linear mind, I want you to consider this with the spherical, intuitive mind – there was a time in the distant past where the people who at that time were embodying on earth had a higher level of collective consciousness than what you see on this planet today. Then there was, as Genesis describes, a point where a critical mass of these people fell into a lower state of consciousness.

The Fall of Man was a fall in the individual and collective consciousness. I will later describe what this fall meant and what the consciousness was that people fell into, but for now the point is that there was a past edenic state, but this was not a physical garden located in a physical location. It was a higher state of the collective consciousness.

Then, there was an event whereby a critical mass of people fell into a lower state of consciousness on an individual basis, and this dragged the collective consciousness down. This fall in the collective consciousness has had a profound effect on all aspects of life on this planet. What I want to focus on here is that the primary effect on human beings has been that people have become blinded to the deeper reality of the Christ mind. I have hinted at this deeper reality by saying that the Christ mind is the unifying link between Creator and creation. It is also what unifies all individual self-aware beings.

Raising yourself above the collective consciousness

The Christ mind shows you the underlying reality that all life is one. You are one with your Creator and you are one with all other individual beings because you are all expressions of the Creator's Being. This is also what makes it possible for you to see that the earth is an energy field and that there is a collective consciousness.

You are part of that collective consciousness. You are affected by that consciousness and you will affect the collective consciousness. You can either allow the collective consciousness to drag you down, or you can pull yourself above the collective consciousness, and thereby you become a magnet for raising the collective consciousness.

My life was meant to demonstrate the path whereby an individual human being can raise him- or herself beyond the level of the collective consciousness. You can reach a higher state where you put on the state of consciousness wherein you recognize the Christ inside yourself. You walk the path that I demonstrated, and therefore you let this mind be in you which was also in Christ Jesus. You realize that you are a son or daughter of God, you realize that you are worthy to manifest your personal Christhood.

What happened in the distant past was that a critical mass of people fell below the Christ consciousness. When I walked the earth 2,000 years ago, I talked about the Christ consciousness as "life" and the lower consciousness as "death." That is why I said: "Let the dead bury their dead." That is why I said that unless you partake of the body and blood of Christ – meaning the Christ consciousness – you have no life in you. The Christ consciousness *is* life.

The illusion of the external church

There came a point where a critical mass of people fell into the consciousness of death. They now became blinded to the reality of oneness, the reality that all life is one and therefore all is one with its source, with its Creator. They became susceptible to the illusion, defined by the Luciferian consciousness, that the world in which you live, the material world, is separated from God and God's kingdom. God is not in this world, and therefore there is a distance between you and God. They became susceptible to the illusion that you cannot cross that distance on your own, and that is why you need an external priesthood, an external church and an external savior.

You need these external authorities to do something for you that you cannot do on your own. This is the essence of the Luciferian lie, and it is an attempt by those who are in the Luciferian consciousness to set themselves up as being the only doorway or the only link between you and God. Look at the Jewish religion 2,000 years ago, and you will see that many of the leaders had set themselves up so that they seemingly had the power to either retain people's sins or forgive peoples sins. This meant that these leaders seemingly had the power to condemn people to hell or take them to heaven.

The people were powerless, and their only chance of salvation was to follow the power elite of the established religion. When you see this, it is not difficult to see that the Christian religion became exactly the same kind of religion. During the so-called Dark Ages most people in Europe believed that the Catholic Church and its hierarchy had the power to take them to heaven or condemn them to an eternity of torment in a fiery hell.

The power elite are as gods on earth

What was the effect? It was that these leaders literally became like gods on earth. Why is this significant? Because when you go back to the story of Genesis, you realize that what the serpent said to Eve was that if she ate of the forbidden fruit, she would become "as a God, knowing good and evil." Can you begin to see the inner, mystical meaning of these words?

There is a truth here. The serpent in the garden can be seen as a representative of both the consciousness of Lucifer and the consciousness of Satan. I will from now on call these two states the "consciousness of anti-christ" because they are truly in opposition to the consciousness of Christ.

Why are they in opposition to the consciousness of Christ? The consciousness of Christ is oneness, but the consciousness of anti-christ opposes oneness, obscures oneness. It is the consciousness of anti-christ that makes you believe, and even experience, that you are separated from God, that the material universe is separated from God's kingdom and that God is not here. What is the deeper effect of this consciousness? What is the deeper meaning behind the statement that you will become

6 | The Inner Meaning of the Fall of Man

as a God, knowing good and evil, when you partake of the forbidden fruit? The forbidden fruit was not a physical fruit, it was the state of consciousness that I have described, the consciousness of anti-christ.

It was "forbidden" in the sense that when you partake of it, you will fall into separation and lose your sense of oneness with your source. We will later talk about why the fruit was even in the garden, but for now I want to stay with the point I am seeking to illustrate.

When you have the consciousness of Christ, you see the underlying oneness of all life; you see that everything sprang from the same source, namely the Creator. There is no distance, there is no separation, there is no division or chasm between you and God. You see that all people on earth are part of the collective consciousness, which is truly the deeper meaning behind the statement to do unto others as you want them to do unto you.

When you see with the Christ mind, you see that since all people are connected with the collective consciousness, whatever you do will either raise the collective consciousness or lower it. Since you are living inside that collective consciousness, you will affect yourself by what you do to others. If you do something that raises the collective consciousness, you will affect yourself positively. If you do something that lowers the collective consciousness, you will affect yourself negatively. This is simply an inevitable realization when you have the Christ mind.

When you fall into the consciousness of anti-christ, you can no longer see this reality. This means you no longer have an objective guiding rod for human behavior. When you see with the consciousness of Christ, it is very simple to evaluate your behavior. Does it raise the collective consciousness, does it raise the energies, does it raise your own individual consciousness or does it lower it? It is a very simple evaluation when you see with the perspective, the single-eyed vision, of the Christ mind.

When you fall into the consciousness of anti-christ, you have a dual vision, a divided vision. You have become a house divided against itself. You have entered a state of consciousness where there is no objective reality. You have become as a god in the sense that in the illusory world of the mind of anti-christ, you seem to have the authority, the capacity and the right to define what is good and evil.

Defining good and evil based on anti-christ

You are "knowing" good and evil in the sense that you are *defining* what is good and what is evil. You are doing so not based on the *objective* vision of the Christ mind. You are doing it based on the *subjective,* dualistic, relative vision of the mind of anti-christ. In the mind of Christ there are no opposites; you see the oneness of all life. In the mind of Christ there is no devil, there is only God. When you see oneness there is no division, and therefore there cannot be anything that opposes God. When you see with the mind of Christ, you see that the devil has no permanent reality, in fact has no reality whatsoever.

I am not thereby saying that there is no such thing as a consciousness of Lucifer and Satan. I am not saying that there are not beings who embody that consciousness to a smaller or larger degree. What I *am* saying is that these beings and the consciousness of anti-christ have no ultimate reality in the Christ mind. They have only a temporary existence, and they seem real only when you look through the filter of the mind of anti-christ.

The Fall of Man was a fall in the level of people's consciousness so that instead of looking at life through the single-eyed vision of the Christ mind, they are now looking at life through the filter of the dualistic vision of the mind of anti-christ. This is what I attempted to explain to people 2,000 years ago, but which it was very difficult to explain because the collective consciousness was lower and people did not have the outer knowledge that you have today, such as the awareness of energy and energy fields. They did not even have the understanding of the human psyche that most people take for granted today.

It was very difficult to describe in words the difference between the mind of Christ and the mind of anti-christ. It has become easier today, but as I have discoursed on earlier, do not think that words can ever capture the fullness of the Christ mind. Words are only meant to help you realize that there is something beyond the consciousness of anti-christ. By striving for it, you can raise your mind above the level represented by the consciousness of anti-christ, and thereby you can come to see the reality of the Christ mind, the reality of oneness.

Because the collective consciousness was so much lower 2,000 years ago, it was inevitable that very, very few people were able to grasp the fullness of my message. I am in no way blaming Peter, nor am I blaming the many other people who were blinded by the same consciousness as Peter. I am not blaming the Emperor Constantine or the early leaders of the Roman Catholic Church.

I am not here to blame. I am here to explain what happened because in today's world the collective consciousness has been raised to the point where many more people can begin to see through the consciousness of anti-christ. They can begin to consciously recognize the difference between Christ and anti-christ and therefore free themselves from the illusions of the consciousness of anti-christ.

7 | CAN CHRISTIANITY FILL PEOPLE'S SPIRITUAL NEEDS?

The question in terms of Christianity becomes whether Christianity will be able to recognize the shift, the raising of the collective consciousness? Will Christianity as an outer institution be able and willing to transform itself based on the fact that the collective consciousness has been raised? If Christianity had already been willing and able to do this, you would not see people leaving Christian churches.

Why are people leaving Christian churches in the more developed part of the world? Because the Christian churches are not meeting the spiritual needs that people have in this age. What are those needs? Well, this will be my next topic.

Two thousand years ago, the majority of the people on this planet were very much trapped at the level of consciousness represented by Peter. They were not able to fully grasp the message of Christ. Many were still able to recognize Christ as having something to offer, but they were not willing to follow Christ all the way to the death of the outer, mortal self, the self that is based on the consciousness of anti-christ. They were not willing to let that mortal self die, to lose that mortal self, in order to be reborn of the fire of the Christ mind, thereby attaining a higher sense of identity. Again, this is not said to blame; it is simply to explain the reality.

It is not surprising that the majority of the people did not understand the deeper aspects of my mission. I was somewhat aware of this when I walked the earth. That is why, even as the scriptures record, I gave my teachings at two different levels. I taught the multitudes in parables, but when we were alone I expounded all things to my disciples.

I gave a general teaching for the broader numbers of people. I gave a more specific teaching for the people who were ready to engage in the path that leads you beyond the consciousness of anti-christ. You put on your personal Christhood by attaining the consciousness of Christ, the Christ mind.

The lower stages of the path to Christhood

If you will look at this honestly, you will see that even the teaching I gave for the public was a teaching that was entirely non-violent. The example I set was non-violent. Even when Peter, in the Garden of Gethsemane, drew his sword and cut off the ear of a Roman soldier, I rebuked Peter and I healed the soldier. When I was put on trial, I did not defend myself. I allowed the Romans to persecute, torture and crucify me.

The message that has not been understood here is that most people were not at a level of consciousness where they could consciously engage in the direct path to Christhood. My outer teaching was therefore meant to give them the tools to raise themselves up to the point where they were able to consciously grasp and engage in this path.

How do you raise yourself from a lower state of consciousness to the point where you can grasp the path of Christhood? You do so *only* by overcoming all tendency to use violence, all tendency to use force, by becoming completely non-violent in your dealings with other people. You are living up to my statement that you stop looking at the splinter in the eyes of your brother, and this is when you become ready to look at the beam in your own eye.

You may think that the path to Christhood is a glorious path, but it is actually the difficult path of looking at the elements of anti-christ in your own consciousness and systematically rising above them by seeing them as the illusions they are and replacing them with the recognition of the Christ mind. This is an *inner* path. It is not a matter of following outer steps; it is a matter of transforming your individual state of consciousness by systematically rooting out the elements of anti-christ and putting on the mind of Christ. You do this step by step, as Paul said: "I die daily." He meant that on a daily basis he saw some illusion of the mortal self and allowed an aspect of the mortal self to die whereby he was purifying his mind from the elements of anti-christ. He was opening his mind to the life of Christ that could enter and become as the leaven that would raise the whole loaf of his consciousness.

At the highest level, I came to give the direct path to the Christ consciousness, but because most people were not ready for this, I gave an outer teaching that would help people prepare for the path to Christhood by becoming non-violent. This means that you can say: "Well, people were not ready for the higher path, and therefore it was understandable that the outer religion of Christianity became influenced by the consciousness of Peter. It was understandable that Christianity as an institution could not teach the higher teaching but taught the lower teaching." This *is* understandable, but *did* Christianity as an institution teach my lower teaching?

Did Christianity ever teach the path of Christ?

My lower teaching was meant to take you from the consciousness that most people were in to a state of consciousness where you have become non-violent. Was the Christian religion non-violent? Has the Christian religion been a force for non-violence in the world? Is the Christian religion today a force for non-violence in the world?

You will see that, almost from the moment of the formation of the Roman Catholic Church, that church took on a more militant, violent and force-based approach. Suddenly, the Christian leaders went from being a persecuted minority to now having the backing of the military might of the Roman Empire. Suddenly, they went from preaching their own message to now seeing it as their job to eradicate all different or conflicting religions. When you look through the Dark Ages and the Middle Ages, you see how the Catholic Church became increasingly violent in the Crusades, the Inquisition, the witch hunts and the persecution of scientists.

When you see this, you cannot say that the Catholic Church taught my lower message. From the very beginning, the Catholic Church began to distort even my outer message. At the same time, it started completely eradicating my higher message of the path to individual Christhood. Instead, it became exactly the same kind of religion as the Jewish religion that persecuted and killed me.

The leaders of the Catholic Church became as gods who defined what was good and evil. They did not define this based on the authority of Christ, based on the Christ mind, based on the vision of oneness. Nay, they defined it exclusively based on the consciousness of anti-christ, and therefore the doctrines and dogmas that they defined were not in alignment with the reality of Christ. They were entirely constructed from the dualistic vision of the mind of anti-christ and they reinforced that state of consciousness.

What I am saying here is the simple reality that I know most Christians will not be willing to hear. The simple reality is that the Christian religion lost both my lower message and my higher message. My true message of transformation to a higher state of consciousness has been completely lost in the Christian religion, and it remains lost to this day by almost every Christian church. *That* is why people in the developed part of the world are leaving the Christian religion.

Today's spiritual people need a path

Many people have raised their individual consciousness to the point where they realize that true spirituality is not about following an outer church, an outer doctrine or even an outer savior. True spirituality is about seeking the kingdom of God within yourself and walking an active path whereby you gradually transform your state of consciousness until you reach a higher state of consciousness, namely the consciousness of Christ.

Many people may not be able to explain this, they may not be aware with their conscious minds. Nevertheless, they feel in their hearts the reality of this, and they are seeking the true path, a valid path, to a higher state of consciousness. As long as the Christian religion cannot meet this spiritual need, it will continue to lose members.

The members it will lose are precisely the people who have the highest level of consciousness and therefore have the highest potential to actually grasp and live the message of Christ. What the Christian religion started doing after the formation of the Catholic Church was to preach the same kind of message that has been preached by many other religions, namely that the kingdom of God is outside yourself and that the key to salvation is found outside yourself.

The lawyers of the Christian religion started denying the Key of Knowledge, which is that the kingdom of God is within you and therefore you can find it only by looking within, by transforming yourself. How do you transform yourself? You stop looking at the splinter in the eye of your brother and you start honestly looking at the beam in your own eye, rooting out those elements of anti-christ. Instead, the Christian religion started preaching the dis-empowering message that you do not have what it takes to save yourself. Therefore, you need an external organization on earth in order to qualify to enter heaven.

There is a subtlety here. You do *not* have what it takes to save yourself within the consciousness of anti-christ, within the mortal self. You *do* have the Key of Knowledge inside of you whereby you can go within and establish an inner contact to the higher Christ mind. Through that inner contact, you can receive the vision that then enables you to root out the elements of anti-christ in your consciousness. This empowers you to raise your state of consciousness beyond the level of anti-christ. You are putting on the mind of Christ and coming to the point where the prince of this world comes and has nothing in you whereby he can pull you into the illusions of anti-christ. He cannot cause you to cling to your mortal sense of life, your mortal sense of identity.

The path has been deliberately removed

This is the path I came to demonstrate. If you are willing to take an objective look at the history of the Christian religion, you will see that this path has not only been lost, it has been systematically, deliberately and aggressively eradicated. What can explain that the true message and the true path of Christ was taken out of the religion that claims to represent Christ on earth? As I have said, there is only one possible explanation: The Christian religion was taken over by the consciousness and the forces of anti-christ. Nothing else can explain that the Christian religion has eradicated the inner path and has even eradicated the outer path by becoming a violent and forceful religion.

How can anyone believe that a person who is in the Christ mind can accept that by torturing and killing another human being, you can save the soul of that human being? No one who has even a glimpse of the Christ mind can believe this. Only people who are completely blinded by the consciousness of anti-christ can believe that anyone can be forced to be saved. The deeper reality is that the key to salvation is your free will, that *you make the choice to be saved*. The choice you are making is not just one choice, it is the many choices whereby you come to see the elements of anti-christ in your own mind.

You choose to dismiss the lies of the devil, the temptations of the serpent, and accept a morsel of the Christ consciousness that replaces it. You die daily by letting a part of your mortal human self – what in modern times is often called the ego – die. You then accept the body and blood as the truth and the light of the Christ consciousness whereby you are reborn into a slightly higher sense of identity than you had yesterday. When you continue to walk this path, there will come a point – for some it will be *after* this lifetime, for others it will be *in* this lifetime – where you have put on a certain level of Christhood and therefore can accept yourself as a son or daughter of God.

This is what Paul had understood, and that is why he said that Christ came into this world to give people the power to become the sons and daughters of God. You are not actually gaining the power to become a son or daughter of God, but you are gaining the power to raise your mind beyond the perception filter of the mind of anti-christ so that you can accept that you always were a son or daughter of God. Without him was not anything made that was made—including *you*.

How Christianity can remain relevant

If the Christian religion is to continue to have relevance in the modern world, it must transform itself. It must restore both the lower and the higher path of Christ. It must transform itself into a religion that does not present a ready-made, instant salvation but a gradual path to a higher state of consciousness. There is absolutely no other way for the Christian religion to be relevant in the times to come.

We have crossed the boundary to a new spiritual cycle. I came to inaugurate one cycle when I took embodiment 2,000 years ago. My embodiment marked the end of the cycle represented by Moses and the escape from Egypt. This was a symbol for a certain level of consciousness. My coming marked that humankind was ready to enter a new spiritual cycle and face a new level of initiation.

What was meant to happen in the past 2,000 years was that people were meant to escape the illusion of the external savior, the external church, the external power elite that holds the key to the salvation or the condemnation of the people. People were meant to recognize and accept that the true key to salvation lies in the kingdom that is within themselves. An outer institution can be helpful, *if* it helps you find what is within yourself. If the outer institution tells you that you do not have anything of value in yourself, but that you need an external savior, then that outer institution is preaching the message of anti-christ. It does not matter that this outer institution calls itself Christianity; it is still preaching the message of anti-christ.

I AM the ascended Jesus Christ. I am giving you a life-giving truth that can set you free from the collective consciousness, the collective beast, that has actually been reinforced by the Christian religion. The Christian movement was meant to set people free from this consciousness, but instead it was transformed into a tool for reinforcing this consciousness.

If you think this is to my liking, you are severely mistaken. In fact, I will make the provocative statement that there is only one thing that can cause you to reject the message I am giving in this book, and it is that you are blinded by the consciousness of anti-christ. This is the exact same mechanism that caused people to reject me when they met me in the flesh 2,000 years ago. They were so blinded by the consciousness of anti-christ that they could not see the Christ light in me.

They believed, in their pride and arrogance, that they were as gods on earth. They had the right to define what was good and evil, what was Christ and anti-christ. They had the right to say that this person walking around Galilee cannot be the promised Messiah, cannot be the Living Christ. Therefore, we have a right to condemn him and have him executed so that he will not stir up the people and question our power over the people. The Christian religion was turned into an institution for the consciousness of anti-christ, the very consciousness that believes that it is as a god on earth and can define good and evil.

Christianity was taken over by anti-christ

The Christian movement was meant to set people free from the consciousness of anti-christ and give them the consciousness of Christ. Instead, the Christian movement became taken over by the consciousness of anti-christ. The leaders of the Christian movement began to believe that they had the right and the capacity to define what was Christ and anti-christ.

This was the consciousness of anti-christ setting itself up as the authority that could define what is Christ and anti-christ. If your definition of Christ and anti-christ is based on the consciousness of anti-christ, do you think you will ever be able to recognize Christ? *Nay, of course you will not!* You will reject Christ and you will cling to the illusions of anti-christ.

This you have a right to do. God has given you free will. Planet earth is one among many planets with self-aware beings. Planet earth is one of the lower planets in terms of the level of the collective consciousness. It is one of a dwindling number of planets where it is still possible for the inhabitants to be completely blinded by the consciousness of anti-christ to the point where they deny the underlying oneness of all life.

They think they are living in a separate world where there is no God and that is not connected to anything outside themselves. They think they are a law unto themselves, they think they can do whatever they want without having any negative effect on themselves.

This is perfectly within the Law of Free Will. It is perfectly within the Law of Free Will that an institution emerged that was entirely based on the consciousness of anti-christ yet made the claim that it had the authority of Christ and was the only true representative of Christ.

This is perfectly within the Law of Free Will, but it is also within the Law of Free Will that I, as an ascended being, challenge this illusion and that I do so through one – and hopefully in the future many – who are willing to make themselves open doors for the truth of Christ.

It was perfectly within the Law of Free Will that when I walked the earth 2,000 years ago, I was an open door for the truth of Christ. I challenged the scribes and the Pharisees, I overturned the table of the moneychangers. I challenged the false leaders of the false outer religion that claimed that it could keep people out of the kingdom of God that is within them.

How can an outer institution, an outer power elite, keep you out of the kingdom of God when the kingdom of God is within you? Can you be a Christian and deny that I said that the kingdom of God is within you?

Can you call yourself a Christian and deny what I have said in this book? If you *can,* then I can only say one thing, the same thing I said to Peter: "Get thee behind me Satan, for thou art an offence to me. Thou savourest not the things that be of God but the things that be of men, the things that be of the relative, dualistic mind of anti-christ." *That* mind I have come to challenge. *That* mind I have come to denounce. *Are you willing to do the same?*

8 | CHRISTIANITY PERVERTED THE CONCEPT OF A SAVIOR

What exactly is the consciousness of anti-christ? When I say the word "anti-christ," it is inevitable that those who hear or read it have an image spring up in their minds. As I have attempted to explain, this image will be influenced by the Christian religion. The Christian religion has now, for many centuries, presented itself as the ultimate authority on the topic of what is Christ and what is anti-christ. Yet the Christian religion was taken over by the consciousness of the anti-christ, and what does that mean?

It means that the consciousness of anti-christ has defined the outer doctrines, teachings and rules that have come to define Christ. Therefore, the consciousness of anti-christ has also defined what people see as anti-christ. *Anti-christ has defined itself.*

This is essential to understand for those who wish to step on to the true path of Christ. The true path of Christ is the path that takes you beyond the consciousness of anti-christ, the consciousness of death. How can you walk that path? You can walk it only when you reach for the direct, inner connection to the consciousness of Christ, which you have access to in the kingdom of God that is within you.

You must use the Key of Knowledge to make a connection to a spiritual being, a spiritual teacher, who is beyond your current state of consciousness, what I have called your mental box or your perception filter.

The outer and the inner path of Christ

Beware of the subtlety here. You *do* need something from outside your current perception filter and mental box because your current state of mind is too influenced by the consciousness of anti-christ. The consciousness of anti-christ is like quicksand. The more you struggle, the deeper you sink into it.

How can you get out of quicksand? Well, first you must lie still. You must stop struggling, you must become non-violent, whereby you stop the movement of sinking deeper and deeper into the quicksand. This, of course, will only stop the downward pull.

The outer path of Christ, that I have talked about, is the one of becoming non-violent. This means that you stop struggling against the consciousness of anti-christ so that you stop yourself from sinking deeper into it. Stopping the sinking movement will not get you out of the quicksand. The only way to get out of the quicksand is that something from outside the system itself must give you a lifeline that you can grab on to and use to pull yourself above the downward pull of the quicksand.

All human beings on earth are currently blinded by the consciousness of anti-christ to a greater or smaller degree, in most cases to a greater degree. You cannot get out of this by using the consciousness of anti-christ. You cannot *reason* your way out of the quicksand, of the quagmire, of the consciousness of anti-christ by using the consciousness of anti-christ.

This is the entire idea of the incarnation, the coming of a savior. God, or rather the ascended masters who are the overseers of the spiritual development of humankind, are quite aware

8 | Christianity Perverted the Concept of a Savior

of what is happening on earth. We know that once people are trapped in the consciousness of anti-christ, they cannot get out of it by their own powers. They do need something from outside themselves in order to start the path that leads them out.

That is why I was sent to earth 2,000 years ago to take physical embodiment. That is why other genuine spiritual teachers have been sent both before and after. That is why many people who are in embodiment today have volunteered to come into embodiment at this critical time in order to embody and demonstrate the Christ consciousness.

The outer savior cannot save you

Even though you need an outer savior to give you a different perspective, it is still not the outer savior that saves you. What the outer savior *can* do is help you use the Key of Knowledge to activate the faculties that are built in to your mind; not the physical brain but the higher mind of your being. What the outer savior *can* do is to help you redirect your attention so that instead of projecting your attention outward, you are now turning it inward, thereby discovering the kingdom of God that is within you.

Do you see what has happened to the Christian religion? It has taken the concept of an outer savior and perverted it so that it now claims that it is the outer savior, and the outer savior alone, who can take you into the kingdom of God.

If the kingdom of God is within you, how can an outer savior take you there? What the outer savior *can* do is help you walk into the inner kingdom, but he cannot do it *for* you. You must do it for yourself with the help of the outer teacher. You must grab on to a lifeline from the Christ consciousness that the outer teacher presents to you. Then you must use that lifeline to pull yourself above the quicksand of the consciousness of anti-christ.

How will you do this? How will you pull yourself above the consciousness of anti-christ? You will do so in only one way, and that is by following one of my most important statements, or at least one of the most important statements incorporated in the official scriptures. That statement is simply this: "Stop looking at the splinter in the eyes of your brothers and sisters and start looking for the beam in your own eye."

In order to enter the kingdom of God that is within you, you have to be willing to look at yourself, your own mind, your own psychology, your own consciousness. You have to be willing to see that you have elements of the consciousness of anti-christ in your own mind. You have to be willing to see what they are, and then you have to be willing to choose life, the life of the Christ consciousness, over the death of the anti-christ consciousness.

You have to choose to leave your nets and follow the Living Christ wherever he takes you. The nets are a symbol for your entanglement with the consciousness of anti-christ, including the collective consciousness on earth as a whole and in your local community, even your family environment. That is why I said that those who love their family more than me are not worthy of me. It does not really mean that they are not worthy, it means that they are not capable of following the Living Christ. In order to follow the Living Christ, you have to be willing to leave behind your nets of entanglements with the collective consciousness that is currently so affected by the consciousness of anti-christ.

How the Living Christ appears

The Living Christ, in whatever form he may appear, always comes to appeal to those who have the potential to raise their individual consciousness beyond the level of the collective consciousness where they live and on the planet as a whole. I have earlier said that what has created the progress in human history

8 | Christianity Perverted the Concept of a Savior

is the raising of the collective consciousness. This raising of the collective consciousness can happen in only one way: By individual human beings raising their individual consciousness and thereby pulling up the whole.

That is why I said: "And I, if I be lifted up from the earth, shall draw all men unto me." If I be lifted up in consciousness, then I create a magnetic pull that raises the whole. In order to create a pull that raises the whole, you have to raise your individual consciousness beyond the collective. This, I trust, should be obvious to anyone who bothers to consider it.

In every age, there is a certain number of people who have the potential to raise their individual consciousness beyond the level of the collective and thereby pull up the collective. These are the kind of people that the Living Christ comes to offer a path beyond the level of the collective consciousness of the time.

What I could do 2,000 years ago was to give people a teaching that was beyond the collective consciousness *at the time*. I could *not* give them a teaching that was too far beyond for they would not have been able to grasp it. Just look at the fact of how the Christian religion has perverted both the outer path and the inner path. Is it not obvious that there was a limit to what I could give people back then? Is it not obvious that the scriptures, that were written down so long ago, cannot in any way represent the ultimate teaching that could be given by the Living Christ? That is why I said: "I have yet many things to say unto you, but you cannot bear them now."

The level of the collective consciousness was not high enough for this teaching to be given. That is why, in this book and in my other teachings, I have given a higher teaching. This reflects the fact that the collective consciousness has indeed been raised over the past 2,000 years. Those in the Christian religion who sit there and say that the official scriptures of Christianity represent the ultimate teaching that could ever be given by Christ are indeed completely blinded by the consciousness of anti-christ. They are denying the Living Christ the opportunity to give a teaching adapted to the level of the collective consciousness as it is today. It is completely against the reality of the Living Christ.

How anti-christ denies Christ in you

How is it possible that people can sit there in their Christian churches and be absolutely convinced that they are right, that the Bible is the infallible word of God and that the Bible represents the ultimate teaching that ever *can* and ever *will* be given by God or by Christ on this planet? It is possible because this is exactly what the consciousness of anti-christ enables people to do.

As I said, the consciousness of anti-christ has managed to define itself. It has defined itself in such a way that people who believe in this definition will never be able to free themselves from the subtler aspects of the consciousness of anti-christ. They will never to be able to actually see or accept the lifeline lowered by the Living Christ, and therefore they will never be able to pull themselves above the quicksand of the consciousness of anti-christ.

What the consciousness of anti-christ has done is to define Christ as something external to yourself and say that it is only through this external savior that you will be saved. It has then identified Christ with one historical person, namely myself, and said that this was the *exclusive* incarnation of Christ that will ever happen on earth.

The deeper reality is that Christ cannot be confined to one historical person. *All* human beings have the potential to put on the mind of Christ and accept the fact that they are sons and daughters of God and that they are the Living Christ in embodiment. I did not come 2,000 years ago to be elevated as a God, a false god, a graven image, an idol, as the exclusive incarnation of Christ. I came to demonstrate the path whereby many other people could become incarnations of Christ to a greater or smaller degree.

How will you ultimately free yourself from the consciousness of anti-christ? By letting Christ incarnate in you, by you becoming the next incarnation of Christ.

9 | CHRISTIANITY HAS TAKEN AWAY JESUS' VICTORY

What is the ultimate success of a teacher? It is that he duplicates himself in his students so that the students reach the same level that he demonstrated, possibly even a higher level. I came to offer people a path whereby those who dare to believe on me would do the same, and even greater, works than I did.

I have not had my victory of seeing a substantial number of people follow both the outer and the inner path to the point where they could accept their personal Christhood and dare to demonstrate it. Why have I not had this victory? Because the forces of anti-christ have taken it away from me. What has been the primary weapon they have used to take away my victory? It has been what calls itself the Christian religion.

In objectifying Christ and identifying him as being outside yourself, what have they also done to anti-christ? They have objectified anti-christ and identified anti-christ as being some being out there away from you. This is what most Christians would call the devil, Satan or Lucifer. They think that there is one being out there who is the embodiment or the incarnation of evil.

Anti-christ is separation from oneness

Again, there is a subtlety. There have been beings who have misused their free will to the extent where they have become completely identified with the consciousness of anti-christ. One can say that they have represented an ultimate incarnation of anti-christ. The entire point of the true teachings of Christ is that Christ is a state of consciousness and anti-christ is a state of consciousness. Christ is the consciousness of oneness. Anti-christ is the consciousness of separation from oneness.

Planet earth is one among many planets with self-aware life forms. Planet earth is one of the lower planets because it is one of a shrinking number of planets that still allows people to embody who are trapped in the consciousness of violence, the consciousness of struggling against other people.

Contrary to the common view promoted by the Christian religion, it is possible to see the consciousness of anti-christ, not as an external force embodied by one being but as a consciousness embodied by many beings. All human beings who are currently embodying on earth are to some degree embodying the consciousness of anti-christ.

I know very well that many people will object to this statement and say that they could not possibly embody the consciousness of anti-christ. They will come up with all kinds of reasonings for this, possibly by referring to their membership of an external religion, their beliefs, their good deeds or this or that or the next thing.

The two tasks of Christ

The simple fact is that if you look at this planet, you will see that there is an incredible amount of atrocities being committed on a daily basis. You cannot look at what is happening on earth and believe that a perfect God created this planet in its current state and that this state represents the best that this perfect God could possibly create.

If you are willing to acknowledge that planet earth is far from the highest potential, you must begin to ask yourself why this is so. Why is it possible that a planet can sink so far below what you know in your heart is the highest potential? If you go into your heart and use the Key of Knowledge to tune in to your own inner knowing, you will know that most of the things that are going on – most of the violence, most of the atrocities, most of man's inhumanity to man – simply are not the way things could be, they are not the highest potential. You must therefore ask yourself why is it possible that a planet can sink so far below the highest potential? How is it possible that humankind as a whole could fall into the lower state of consciousness, the consciousness of anti-christ? This is possible because of free will.

I have in other books given more extensive teachings on this so what I will give here is only a short version. The fact of the matter is that the purpose of your existence as an individual being is your growth in consciousness. As I said 2,000 years ago when challenged by the scribes and Pharisees, there is an old scripture which says: "Yea are Gods." You are a God in the making.

You have been created with a localized sense of identity, a localized sense of self. By taking embodiment on earth, you have been given the opportunity to expand your localized sense of self. When you expand your localized self to a certain degree, you will no longer want to embody on earth. You will qualify for the process that I demonstrated, namely the process whereby you permanently ascend to the spiritual realm. Once you have ascended and become an ascended master, you can continue to raise your consciousness until you reach the same level of awareness as the Creator who created you out of its own Being.

This is your ultimate potential. All human beings are walking the path whereby, through their free-will choices, they raise their consciousness. How do you raise your consciousness? You raise your consciousness by coming to the realization: "Oh, I now see that I have certain elements in my own consciousness that are limiting me, that are restricting me. I see that I have created a self that is based on an illusion of separation from my source and from the whole. I see that this separate self is limiting me and I am letting that self die so that I can be reborn into a higher sense of self."

This is what it means to follow Christ. You are, at this moment, in a certain state of consciousness where you see life and yourself through a particular self. There is not necessarily anything wrong or evil about this self, but it is not your highest potential. If it had been your highest potential, you would not be in embodiment on a planet like earth.

Christ comes to you to first give you the realization that there is something beyond your present self. There is *more*. It is possible, as a human being, to be more than you are right now. This is what even Peter saw in me. He saw that I was more than he was; I had a higher sense of self than he had. The first task of Christ is to actually awaken people to the fact that they do not have to be confined to the kind of self they have right now and the kind of self that most people have in their environment, even the level of self that most people have on earth right now. There is more, there is a higher potential.

Until people see this, they will think that they simply have to be like everyone else around them. They have been brought up, they have been programmed, to think that this is all there is to being a human. The first task of Christ is to awaken people from this sleep, from this state of death where they think this is all there is.

The next stage of Christ is the most critical. It is to help you realize that if you are to follow Christ into a higher sense of self, you must stop trying to change other people. You must look at the beam in your own eye and focus all of your attention on changing yourself. Do you see how the Christian religion has taken a complete detour by making people focus on converting all people on earth to the Christian religion instead of converting themselves to the true Christian religion, the inner path of overcoming your own limited self, the elements of anti-christ in your consciousness?

Your sense of self can become a closed circle

Free will reigns supreme. The purpose of life is that you grow in consciousness, expanding your sense of self from a localized to a universal, even a cosmic, sense of self. How do you do this? By making choices!

You come to the realization: "I have a certain sense of self, it is limiting me and I am choosing to let it die and be reborn into a higher sense of self. I am choosing to look at the beam in my own eye, I am choosing to look at the elements of anti-christ that are defining my limited, separate self. I am choosing to dismiss them and instead accept the higher reality of Christ that I see." This is the true path of Christ.

From a greater cosmic perspective, one can say that it truly is a matter of the free-will choices of the individual lifestream. You are on the path that leads you to a higher sense of self. How do you walk that path? When you start out the path, you cannot actually see where the path ends. You start out with a localized sense of awareness. You can see that there is something beyond that, but you cannot see too far beyond. You are walking a path, but the path is winding and you cannot see what is around the next bend, you only see a few steps ahead.

The way you walk the path is that you take on a certain sense of self; you live out that sense of self for a certain time. After you have lived that sense of self for a time, you start feeling uneasy, you start feeling restricted, you start feeling like maybe there is more to life than this. It is when you come to this point that you become open to the Living Christ giving you an impulse to grow beyond your current sense of self.

How do you grow? You grow by taking on a certain sense of self and identifying yourself with it, identifying yourself *as* a limited, separate being. Here is the crucial understanding that has been completely taken out of Christianity and almost every other religion on this planet. The crucial understanding is that *any* sense of self that you take on can become a closed circle, a closed box, from which you cannot escape unless you reach for, unless you open your mind to, a higher impulse from the mind, the universal mind, of Christ.

You first identify yourself completely with a certain self, but then you must come to the realization that: "This cannot be all that I am. It must be possible for me to be more than this." When you come to that point, you are open to an impulse from the Christ mind that shows you that there is more. If you take what is given from the Christ mind, in whatever form it appears to you, and if you multiply what you have received, then you can rise to a higher sense of self. In order to rise to that higher sense of self, you must come to see your limited sense of self from the outside. This means that you are no longer fully identified with it.

The self colors your perception

I have talked about perception filters that are like wearing colored glasses. Once you put on the glasses, they color the way you see everything. If you can step outside of the glasses, you see that they were just that: a coloring you had taken on, a filter you had taken on. So it is with your sense of self.

As long as you are *inside* the self, it colors the way you see everything. That is why you must use your built-in ability to mentally step outside your current sense of self, see it from the outside and realize: "I am *more* than this self, and that is why I can take the crucial step of letting my limited self die, knowing through the Christ mind that *I* will not die. I will not cease to exist. I will be reborn into a higher sense of self."

This is what is meant by the statement: "If you seek to save your life, you shall lose it." If you seek to save your separate self, you will lose the life that is following Christ. You will condemn yourself to taking another round being completely identified with that self. Only if you are willing to lose your life for the sake of following Christ, will you be reborn into a higher sense of self.

This does not mean that you are instantly reborn into the ultimate sense of self because the path has numerous stages. You cannot instantly jump from your current sense of self to that of the full Christ consciousness. You must take many different steps. You must, as Paul said, "die daily." You let a part of your separate self die every day and you are reborn daily.

When you have become conscious of this process, then you can accelerate it greatly by being willing to constantly let the Living Christ expose to you certain elements of the consciousness of anti-christ in your own being. You can make surprisingly quick progress in just a matter of years. You can raise your consciousness so that when you look back at your current level of consciousness, you will scarcely believe that you are the same person. Indeed, you are *not* the same person. You are a new person in Christ; you have been spiritually reborn out of the fire of Christ.

The universal definition of anti-christ

What is the consciousness of anti-christ? You are right now in a certain state of consciousness. In reality, you are a formless spiritual being. *Formless*—take note of the word. You are beyond any form. Your current sense of self has form; it is defined in the world of form. You, the formless spiritual being, have forced your formless spirit into this form-based self. You have come to believe that this is who you are, this is all you are, this is all you could ever be. What is it that makes it possible for a formless spiritual being to come to identify itself as a specific form and think this is all there is to your existence? What makes this possible is the consciousness of anti-christ.

It is possible to say that the consciousness of anti-christ is not necessarily a devil who is evil and who is out to do the opposite of God. In its most universal sense, the consciousness of anti-christ is simply what makes it possible for a formless spirit to identify with form, with a form-based self. This is only the most universal definition of the consciousness of anti-christ. There are many more specific definitions, and I will talk about those later.

What makes it possible that a formless spirit can come to believe that a certain form-based self is all there is to its existence and potential? It is a quality of the consciousness of anti-christ, which is the fact that the consciousness of anti-christ is based on a division.

The consciousness of Christ is the consciousness of oneness. I realize full well that when I say this, you are not able to grasp with your outer mind what this truly means. If you were able to grasp it with the outer mind, you would be in the consciousness of Christ and you would not need my explanation in the form of words. I am, in a sense, attempting the impossible of describing a reality to you through words that cannot in any way be confined to words. The consciousness of Christ cannot be adequately described through words. Why not? Because the consciousness of Christ is a total, immersive experience of oneness.

There is a simple example to illustrate this. You can take the best poets in the world and have them give the most elaborate poetic description of a sunset. You may have a person who has never seen a sunset read this description and the person may be stirred and moved by the description. No matter how good the description is, it is not the same as if the person is actually standing on the beach, experiencing the sunset as a total immersive experience. I trust you can see with the outer mind that there is a difference between description and experience.

Why it is so difficult to escape anti-christ

The tricky part of the consciousness of anti-christ is that once you step into it, once you eat of that forbidden fruit, you can no longer experience the fullness of the consciousness of Christ, which means what? It means you must now settle for a *description* of the consciousness of Christ.

The consciousness of *Christ* is the total experience of oneness. The consciousness of *anti-christ* is where you experience everything through a filter of concepts, ideas or words. The consciousness of *Christ* is the total experience; the consciousness of *anti-christ* is a *description* of the experience. In the consciousness of Christ, you are immersed in oneness. In the consciousness of anti-christ, you are experiencing everything from a distance, through a filter. There is a filter inserted between your conscious mind and whatever you experience.

Right now, you are sitting, reading this book, experiencing the book, my words, your environment and yourself. You think that the experience you are having is real. You think it shows you the way the world really is. You think this is a real immersive experience. In reality, it is not an immersive experience.

You are experiencing everything through a filter, and that filter is constructed from the consciousness of anti-christ, the consciousness of separation from oneness. This is the most difficult thing to explain for a spiritual teacher because it is the most difficult thing for people to grasp. Some students will grasp this with the linear, logical mind. They see that there is logic here. They realize that their senses, for example, can be fooled and do not give them an accurate experience of reality. Many people realize that when you go outside, you see that the sun is moving around the earth. In reality, your senses are being fooled, and the earth is rotating around itself, making it appear as if the sun is moving. Some students *can* grasp the statement that the consciousness of anti-christ does not show them reality and that their present experience does not show them the fullness of reality.

How can you grasp exactly how different is the consciousness of anti-christ from the consciousness of Christ when all you have seen is the perception filter created by the consciousness of anti-christ? How can you truly grasp what it is like to experience the world without this filter? It is almost impossible.

You cannot truly grasp this with the outer mind, but you can come to *experience* it in glimpses. This is what has been called a mystical or spiritual experience. Most of the people who will be able to grasp and accept what I am saying here have had such mystical experiences and are to some degree aware of it. If you have had no such experience, what I say here will just be a theory, and your mind will already have constructed arguments against it. This is the very central feature that makes the consciousness of anti-christ so difficult to escape once you are in it.

Opposites and value judgments

The consciousness of anti-christ is based on a division. How do you divide oneness? As an example, take a piece of paper and draw a circle. You have a line that is closed. Now imagine that you cut the circle in one spot and you unfold the circular line into a straight line. Now you have a line that has a clear definition in space. It has two ends; they are at opposite ends of the line. You have now divided the unbroken circle of oneness into a line with two opposite ends.

This is what the consciousness of anti-christ does to everything, but it does more than this. In any topic you can possibly come up with, the consciousness of anti-christ defines two opposites. On top of this, the consciousness of anti-christ adds a value judgment, which says that one opposite is true and the other is false, one is *good* and the other is *evil*. Once you have stepped into this perception filter, you have lost oneness. You have created an artificial view of the world. What have I said previously? Without him was not anything made that was made. God is in everything.

I have talked about you walking a path to God-hood. You start this path with a localized sense of self, and you cannot accept that God is where you are. That is why you must see God as being somewhere "out there." You experience yourself *as* the very localized sense of self. You realize that God is more than this, and therefore you cannot accept that God is within you.

The reason you cannot accept that God is within you is that your formless spirit has stepped into a localized, separate self. The process of growing in self-awareness is that you let go of the local self. Then you are reborn into another local self that is slightly broader. You let go of *that,* and you are reborn again. This continues until you have expanded your sense of self to the point where you can accept that God is within you and that God's kingdom is within you. God's kingdom is a state of consciousness that you can now step into and accept as your true identity.

This process is guided by your free will. The question is: "How long do you have to identify yourself as a being who is separated from God before you can let that identity die and accept yourself as a being who is one with God and one with the all of the Body of God, meaning all other people and even the planet upon which you live?"

The two ways to grow

What is illustrated by the story of the Garden of Eden is that there are two ways to grow. The Garden of Eden illustrates an environment where you, as a localized being, have access to a spiritual teacher who represents the consciousness of Christ. This spiritual teacher is giving you a constant lifeline that is always there, that you can physically see, hear or feel. It is similar to when you are in school here on earth. You are in a physical classroom, there is a teacher standing there and he is giving you instructions that you can physically hear. There is no sense of distance from the teacher or sense that you have to guess what he is saying. You are clearly hearing what he is saying and you can ask him questions.

The Garden of Eden was such a learning environment where new lifestreams with a localized sense of self had constant access to a teacher representing the Christ consciousness. What was the forbidden fruit? It was a state of consciousness where you have now become so immersed in the consciousness of anti-christ that you no longer have a direct connection to the teacher who represents Christ. You have stepped so far into the perception filter of anti-christ that you simply cannot see and hear the teacher.

This means you are now on your own. You are in a self-created environment where you have shut out the teacher. Once you step into that environment, there is no way out from inside the environment. Once you have taken on this most dense version of the perception filter of anti-christ, you cannot take any of the things you can see and use them to reason your way out.

The only way out is that you actually use your reasoning ability to say: "This is not getting me anywhere. I am going around in circles." You will note that there are people who have walked in the desert for many, many hours and there is no landmarks, only flat sand. Suddenly, they find a set of footsteps and they think: "Ah, if I follow those, I will get to my destination." They follow the set of footsteps, and after some time another set of footsteps appears. They keep following them until they realize that they are following their own footsteps because they have walked in a circle.

This you can come to feel, and then you can open yourself up to saying: "There must be something outside my own self-created perception filter, and I want to reconnect to that teacher who represents the Christ consciousness." At that moment, there is a cosmic law which says that when the student is ready the teacher must appear and offer the student a lifeline. This is the first step where the Christ appears in some form or another

Anti-christ can validate any viewpoint

By saying that the only way the Christ could ever appear on earth was as a historical person, called Jesus and living 2,000 years ago, Christianity has denied the very fact that the Living Christ can appear in many different ways to many different people in many different situations. The moment one person – no matter where they live, no matter what is their local environment – is open to something beyond his or her perception filter, then the Living Christ in the form of some kind of teacher will appear to that student.

The Living Christ appears as a representative of a higher state of consciousness, a higher sense of self. It may be in an outer teaching; it may be that the Living Christ appears through an outer religion that is not Christianity. People in both the Hindu, the Buddhist, the Muslim and the Jewish religion have received an impetus from the universal Christ consciousness through a particular religion or someone who represented that religion but had a higher state of consciousness than themselves. The crucial question is whether the person will receive what is offered, will multiply the talents rather than burying them in the ground.

Will the person use it to let the old self die and be reborn? What is it that might prevent people – and that *has* prevented so many people – from multiplying what they have been given? It is the central feature of the consciousness of anti-christ, which is this: Once you are in the consciousness of anti-christ you can *always* validate *any* viewpoint you want and you can refute any viewpoint you want. The consciousness of anti-christ is entirely *relative*. No matter what you want to validate, you can always find reasons and arguments within the consciousness of anti-christ for validating that viewpoint.

I know this requires contemplation, but here is the key understanding. The consciousness of anti-christ is entirely *relative,* but it presents itself as being completely *absolute.* The consciousness of anti-christ creates a viewpoint, an idea or a thought system. This thought system is completely based on a relative perspective of wanting to validate a certain viewpoint, but it is presented as if it is the absolute and infallible truth. What the Catholic Church Fathers did, after Constantine gave them power, was to create a thought system that was almost entirely based on the consciousness of anti-christ. Then, they elevated it to the status of being the absolute truth based on the authority of Christ.

How does the consciousness of anti-christ manage to take a relative "truth" and elevate it to the status of being an infallible truth? It does so because it has created two opposites, a division between what is defined as *true* and what is defined as *false*. In any belief system found on earth, any thought system found on earth, there will be certain statements or axioms that are considered to be self-evidently true or that are considered to be given by an ultimate authority. In any case, these statements are considered to be beyond questioning. What happens in this process is that you take a certain relative "truth" and you elevate it to the status of being beyond questioning. Any idea which contradicts or goes beyond what you have defined as the absolute truth, can automatically be dismissed as being false. Can you see that it is now just a matter of how you define your absolute truth, and then you can validate anything you want?

Anti-christ makes it easy for people to reject Christ

What have I said about the consciousness of anti-christ? It enables you to validate anything you want, but more than that it enables you to validate any self that you have taken on. It makes you believe that you *are* this self and that all there is to you is this self.

What have I said about free will? You are walking a path, and part of this path is that you take on a certain sense of self. You identify yourself fully with it for a time until you have had enough of experiencing yourself through that sense of self. What is it that allows you to identify yourself fully with a form-based and very limited sense of self? It is the consciousness of anti-christ, which excludes *any* hint and idea that there could be more to you than your current sense of self. It immediately defines it as untrue, unreal, possibly even as a dangerous idea coming from the devil.

I know for a fact that there are many Christians who, if they ever read this book, would instantly label my words as coming from the devil, as being a very clever ruse from the devil to ensnare them into giving up their Christian sense of self. They will say, as the scribes and Pharisees did to me 2,000 years ago, that *I* am of the devil. My words are coming from the serpentine mind, aimed at deceiving them into giving up what they know to be the unquestionable truth defined by the Christian religion.

I can only bow to their free will and say: "If you really need to experience yourself through that separate sense of self for another length of time, then that is your choice and it is your right to make that choice. However, I, as the Living Christ, will not let that stop me from speaking my truth. Neither will I condemn you for rejecting me."

I will stand ever-ready to help you when you come to the point where you have had enough of this limited sense of self, where you see how it is restricting you and where you cry out: "There must be more to me than this." At that moment, I will appear to you in whatever form you can accept.

The challenge of truth

One of the great challenges on earth is the question of truth. I have said that once you have stepped into the perception filter of anti-christ, there is no way out of it from inside the filter. You *must* have something from outside the filter. The problem is that there are people who have had a mystical, inner experience of a higher state of consciousness and there are people who have not had this experience. That is why I said that, even 2,000 years ago, I taught an outer and an inner path, a lower and a higher path.

Those who have not had the inner, mystical experience, those who are not ready for the inner path, how do you help these lifestreams? You help them by giving them an outer teaching, an outer religion, an outer system that they can follow. These people are in a state of consciousness where they need to believe that this outer religion has given them a truth that is reliable and that if they keep following it, it will raise their state of consciousness and bring them closer to salvation.

I am not come here to invalidate the Christian religion in its entirety. It may seem as if that is what I am doing, but that is only because you look at my words through the perception filter that sees everything as black and white where something must be either fully in alignment with your truth or it is completely false. I recognize that there is a need for an outer religion that makes the claim that it has a valid teaching and that if people follow it, it brings them closer to salvation. The question is: "Does the current religion of Christianity actually bring people closer to salvation?" The answer is that it totally depends on whether people transcend what I have called the consciousness of violence and struggle or whether they become more entrapped in it.

Christianity does not teach the true path of Christ

The reality is that there is no clear-cut answer to this question. There are Christian denominations in the world where quite a number of the members are internalizing the outer teaching and the outer religion to the point where it is indeed raising their consciousness, making them less violent.

There are also people within those same denominations who are actually using the very same teaching, the very same outer structure, to become more trapped in the consciousness of violence and struggle. That is because there is currently no Christian denomination that teaches the true path of Christ, neither the lower nor the higher path.

This is why I am giving this teaching in the hope that *some* will understand, and some will take this and be willing to create churches that do teach the path. I am not saying that there is only one way to do this. I am not come here to set up this messenger or this teaching as the infallible guideline for how a Christian church should be organized.

I have no problem with many different Christian churches and denominations, as long as they all teach an open-ended message; as long as they all teach that the goal of being a Christian is to walk a path to a higher state of consciousness. This is a gradual path whereby you must look at the beam in your own eye and you must overcome the elements of anti-christ in your being, gradually putting on the mind of Christ. This can be done in many different ways that are adapted to different cultures, different types of people, different levels of consciousness. There is not just one way to do this.

The question is: "Is the church teaching an open-ended path to a higher state of consciousness or is it promoting the fallacy of the external savior?" The external savior is entirely a creation of the mind of anti-christ. It may be supported by bold claims to absolute authority, but they are nothing but the empty posturings of those who have no life in them. They are nothing but the empty posturings of the false pastors, the wolves in sheep's clothing, those who appear beautiful outward but inward they are empty and filled with the bones of dead doctrines, dead beliefs, that have no reality in the truth of Christ.

I am the Living Christ. I am giving you an outer teaching, but I have no desire to have you elevate that teaching to some infallible doctrine. I give you the teaching in words only because I want to give you the desire to step beyond the words and the teaching to a direct experience of the Living Christ. I am giving you a teaching that says that you are capable of having that experience and that this experience is the *only* way to escape the quicksand of the consciousness of anti-christ.

It is the only true path to salvation, to being in the kingdom of God. There is no substitute, regardless of what the false pastors of this world claim, be they in the Christian religion or in any other thought system. You will *never* enter the kingdom of God as long as you retain a perception filter based on the consciousness of anti-christ.

The kingdom of God is an immersive experience of oneness. As long as you see the kingdom of God and yourself through the filter of the consciousness of separation, you cannot accept yourself as being in the kingdom of God. You cannot come into oneness through the consciousness of separation. It is more impossible than for a camel to go through the eye of the needle.

10 | EXPOSING THE CONSCIOUSNESS OF ANTI-CHRIST

I have said that you should not take anything literally and that it is important to understand the hidden symbolism behind the Bible, including the accounts of my life. What then is the hidden symbolism behind the fact that I was born in a manger, that I was born under humble circumstances, that I was born to parents who did not have riches or any standing or position in society? What is the hidden symbolism there? It is that the Living Christ can appear in any form. It is that there was, from an outer perspective, nothing special about me or my parents or the circumstances in which I was born and grew up. This is to set myself up as an *example* not as an *exception*. Most other people have not been born in special circumstances, but you still have a Christ potential.

Beyond this, there is an even deeper symbolism. I have said that the consciousness of anti-christ sets itself up as a god and defines what is good and what is evil. The consciousness of anti-christ defines what is Christ and what is not Christ. One aspect of this is that the consciousness of anti-christ defines a "standard of perfection." This is an other-worldly, superhuman standard that is deliberately defined so that no human being could ever live up to it.

It then applies this standard to anything coming from the spiritual realm, and it says that this thing coming from the spiritual realm must live up to its self-defined standard or it cannot be genuine. This is precisely what the leaders of the Jewish religion had done concerning the coming Messiah. They had created a super-human standard of perfection that the Messiah was supposed to live up to. Because I, in my incarnation as Jesus, did not live up to their standard, they felt justified in rejecting me.

There will never come a perfect Messiah

There are many Jews who today, 2,000 years later, are still waiting for the coming Messiah for they are not willing to recognize that the Messiah they expect will never come. There will never come anything from the spiritual realm that will live up to their standard of perfection. Do you understand why this is so?

The standard of perfection that human beings have created is defined by the mind of anti-christ. Once you accept this standard and accept that it is an absolute standard of perfection that comes from the highest authority, you are trapped in the most closed mental box available on earth.

Why does the Christ come into this world? To set you free from your mental box! How can the Christ set you free by *conforming to* your mental box? If I had come and conformed to the mental box of the Jews at the time, I would have validated their mental box, thus making them even more imprisoned in it than they were before. When the Living Christ comes into this world, he will always challenge the standard of perfection that people have in their culture, in their religion.

When I walked the earth in a physical body 2,000 years ago, I had to challenge the standard of perfection created by the

Jewish religion. Today, as I speak through this messenger, and as we of the ascended masters seek to get our message across to many people, we must again violate the standard of perfection. I am fully aware that many Christians, especially many Christian preachers and leaders, will reject this book. Many will look at the human messenger, find some imperfection and say that this person could not possibly be a genuine messenger for the real Jesus. Others will say that the real Jesus could not possibly have anything to say in today's age for supposedly what was given in the scriptures was the perfect revelation that will stand for all time. This is perfectly in accord with the Law of Free Will.

Why doesn't God prove he exists?

There are many people in today's world who have created a standard of perfection based on materialism, which defines God out of existence. Many religious people have a question deep within their minds of why God has not given an undeniable proof that he exists. Many Christians expect that, one day, I will come back in a fiery apparition in the heavens that will be undeniable for all people. Therefore, all people will be forced to recognize that they, in their own little Christian sects, were the only ones who had the true vision of Christ.

This is the dream of the human ego and its quest for superiority. It is a dream that will never be fulfilled, for the simple reason that on planet earth free will reigns supreme. One aspect of this is that there must always be "plausible deniability." There will come a time when the collective consciousness has been raised to the point that it becomes very difficult to deny the existence of God and the spiritual side to life. At that point, there will be a shift, a quantum leap, to where it will be impossible to deny the spiritual side of life. What you have today, where so many people deny this, will no longer be possible on this planet. Those lifestreams who want to continue to deny it, will then have to go to some other planet or some other realm where deniability is still possible.

For the foreseeable future, plausible deniability will be a law on earth. This means it must be possible to deny that God exists, it must be possible to deny the Living Christ when he appears in whatever form. *I am the Living Christ.* I am appearing to you through this book, but according to the law it must be possible for you to deny this. I am sure that the outer religion of Christianity will be one of the primary means that people will use to deny my apparition in this book.

This is as it should be according to the greater law, the Cosmic Law of Free Will. I fully respect that law. This does not mean that I, Jesus Christ, am in approval of the fact that the religion that claims to represent me on earth is the primary means for denying my apparition on earth. On the one hand, I respect the law, but this does not mean that I need to be happy and content with what people do in my name. If you think I am happy over people being killed in the name of Christ, then you are mistaken. It can only be the consciousness of anti-christ that makes it possible for people to deny Christ in whatever form he appears.

Perfectionism is a creation of anti-christ

Perfectionism is a creation of the consciousness of anti-christ, not a creation of Christ. This is a statement that many Christians will deny because they have been programmed to believe that Christ must have been perfect. They even think that when I appeared on earth, I was perfect. So many Christians today have grown up with this idolized image of Jesus. They see this beautiful drawing of a person in perfectly clean clothing who walks around with a halo around his head. This was not reality, my beloved. I was in a physical body. When I had walked the dusty roads all day, I smelled as bad as any other person. I had certain behaviors and habits, even my looks, that many people disapproved of. This was deliberately done to give them plausible deniability. Only those who will look beyond outer appearances and their own standard of perfection, will be able to recognize the Living Christ for he will always appear in a form that draws the disapproval of many.

The Living Christ will always appear in a form that draws the disapproval of the collective consciousness in the society and culture where he appears. Look at how many people today will say that it is insane to think you can be the open door and take a dictation or a message from the ascended Jesus Christ. They will reject the entire idea of this book outright. Many Christians will look at the book and find one little thing, or even several things, that they disagree with because it contradicts their doctrines. They will use that as an excuse for rejecting the entire book, the entire message, and rejecting that it could be I, the ascended Jesus Christ, who is the originator of the message.

Again, this is as it should be. Yet let me state clearly that I have nothing to do with the form of Christianity that denies me, that denies me as the Living Presence who has the right to speak a message in this day and age through whomever is willing to be the open door. Certainly, you can see that the leaders of the Christian religion are not willing to be the open door for the Living Christ, despite their claims to authority. This is another aspect of this standard of perfection that has been created.

The power elite that denies Christ

I said earlier that no human being can live up to the standard, and this is, of course, true. Yet there has always been the creation of the myth, the appearance, that *some* human beings *are* living up to it, or at least they are above the population. I have said that the Living Christ always challenges the collective consciousness where he appears, but he also challenges the power elite where he appears. Why did I challenge the scribes and Pharisees? Why did I challenge the moneychangers in the Temple and the Temple Priests? Why did I challenge the power elite of the Jewish society? It was because this power elite is actually the primary embodiment of the consciousness of anti-christ. I have talked about the consciousness of anti-christ in general terms. I will now talk about it in more specific terms, in terms of beings – embodied and disembodied – who embody the consciousness of anti-christ to an almost ultimate degree.

We have, through this messenger, given extensive teachings on the fact that there are some beings who have fallen into the consciousness of anti-christ but who did not do it here on earth. I earlier talked about Genesis being a symbol for the fall to a lower state of consciousness where you are blinded by the appearance, the illusion, of separation. There are some beings that fell into this consciousness in a different realm, in a different sphere. These beings could not ascend with the rest of the beings in their sphere, and thus they fell into a lower realm. They have fallen, some of them through many different realms, until they ended up embodying on earth. They were allowed to embody on earth only because the inhabitants of earth in the distant past had fallen into such a low state of consciousness that these fallen beings, sometimes called fallen angels, were allowed to embody here.

These are beings who embodied the consciousness of anti-christ to a very high degree, meaning that they are so identified with it that they simply cannot see how blinded they are. They believe they are superior to any being on earth, including the Living Christ in embodiment. They believe they have a right to set themselves up as the leaders of the people on earth. They are blind and that is why I referred to them as the "blind leaders." They are blind precisely because they are so identified with the consciousness of anti-christ that there is almost no way for them to recognize Christ when he appears before them, even when he appears in the flesh.

Do you think the Sanhedrin and the scribes and the Pharisees could recognize the Christ in me? Do you think the Roman authorities could recognize the Christ in me, even though Pontius Pilate saw something that he could not define or understand. Most of them were so blinded that they did not for a moment entertain the idea that I could be the Messiah, that I could be the Living Christ. They simply considered me dangerous because I preached a message that undermined their authority over the people. They did what they have always done. Given that they have no respect for people on earth, they simply got rid of me.

Dividing people into superior and inferior

What you need to understand here is that the consciousness of anti-christ is the consciousness of separation. This means that you create a division into at least two, but possibly more than two. You see this in humankind, how there are divisions created in many societies. In India, for example, you have had the caste system with the division into four groupings. Many other societies, in fact most societies even today, have a similar division between those who are at the bottom, those who are at the top and those who are somewhere in between. There may be any number of groupings in a society.

What the consciousness of anti-christ also does is to impose a value judgment so those who are at the bottom are of lesser or no value compared to those who are at the top. *They* are of infinite value and clearly superior to the rest of the people. The more you become identified with the consciousness of anti-christ, the more you believe this division is real. What have I said earlier: "Without him was not anything made that was made." God is within everything. Christ is within everything.

Every human being on earth is a son or daughter of God and is an extension of the very Being of the Creator.

You have self-awareness because there is a core of your being, the Conscious You, that is an extension of the Creator's being. This is of infinite value, meaning it is incomparable. There is absolutely no point in the Christ consciousness where there is a comparison, saying that one son or daughter of God is more valuable than another son or daughter of God. This kind of comparison can exist only in the consciousness of anti-christ, in the consciousness of separation and division. The more you become identified with the consciousness of anti-christ, the more you want to set yourself up as being superior to others.

With the consciousness of anti-christ, you can justify absolutely anything you want. If you look at planet earth and see that there is a certain group of lifestreams on earth who originated on this planet, who took embodiment for the first time on this planet, then you will see that these people have a certain sense of commonality and solidarity with each other. They generally do not consider themselves to be superior to others or that certain people from their group are superior to others.

Those who have set themselves up as the superior leaders on earth are precisely the beings who came here after having fallen in a different realm. They have fallen several times, and therefore they have become so identified with the consciousness of anti-christ that they are absolutely convinced of their own superiority.

This means what? It means they consider themselves fundamentally superior to most of the people on earth. They believe they have the absolute, God-given or nature-given, right to do whatever they want with most of the people on earth. They have no inherent respect for most people and certainly not for the people outside their own group, their own *superior* group.

11 | HOW DARK FORCES CONTROL CHRISTIANITY

If you will take an honest look at history, you will see that the history of this planet cannot be understood without realizing the existence of this power elite who have a fundamental belief in their own superiority. You can look at history and see how many times a small elite has acted as if the lives and the rights of the general population meant nothing to them. It *did* mean nothing to them. They saw no value in human life, they saw no value in the individuality of the so-called common people.

The common people are there to serve them, and they have no other purpose. I they refuse to submit, if they refuse to serve as the worker bees to create a privileged lifestyle for the elite, then they must be eradicated, exterminated, as if they were pests. You cannot understand the history of this planet unless you recognize that such a power elite exists and has existed throughout known history—and even further back into what is currently unknown.

This is the current dynamic on planet earth. When you understand this, you recognize that when the Living Christ takes embodiment, the Living Christ becomes the ultimate threat to the power elite on earth. This power elite will do absolutely anything possible to prevent the emergence of the Living Christ in any form. That is why there is some truth to the stories in the scriptures of how King Herod attempted to kill the Christ child, even based on a rumor of my birth. He was willing to kill all male babies in order to eradicate the one that he knew was a threat to his reign. There is some truth to the absolute ruthlessness in the willingness to shut the Living Christ out from this world.

Of course, things have in some parts of the world progressed in the past 2,000 years. You have seen the emergence of societies that recognize human rights as having a fundamental, inviolable value. This has made it much more difficult for the power elite to physically kill the Living Christ. They are still doing everything in their power to kill the Living Christ psychologically, spiritually, and prevent anyone from following in my footsteps, learning from my example, claiming their own Christhood and thereby doing the works that I did and greater works.

What does it mean to do greater works than Jesus Christ? It means that you are able to bring forth something that could not be brought forth 2,000 years ago because the collective consciousness was not ready for it. What you are reading in this book is an example of one person who has been willing to claim his personal Christhood to the point where he can be the open door for bringing forth this message. This is far beyond the teaching I could give when I appeared in a physical body 2,000 years ago. This is an example of doing greater works in today's age.

You do not need to walk on water or perform physical miracles, you need to bring forth teachings that open people's understanding to the reality of Christ. These are the greater works that are needed in this age, not the miracles that were only meant for a lower state of consciousness. What you need to recognize is that when you dare to claim your Christhood, you *will* be attacked by the planetary forces of anti-christ. That is why I wish to give a discourse on these forces.

The four levels of the material realm

In order to understand the forces of anti-christ, you need to understand that the material universe has four levels or layers. What you see with your physical senses represents the lowest layer, which means that it is made from energy of the lowest or most dense vibration. As you know from science, everything is energy, and you can set up a scale from lower vibrations to higher vibrations.

The scale I wish to define here is that the material universe, the physical world, represents the lowest or most dense vibration. When you go much higher, you reach the spiritual realm, which has substantially higher vibrations than the material world. Even in the spiritual realm, you can continue to go to higher and higher vibrations until you reach the level of the Creator. That is why even the Bible talks about a seventh heaven, indicating that there would be six other layers of the heaven world. In reality, there are many more but that is irrelevant to this topic.

Between the physical world and the spiritual realm are three other divisions, three divisions of the material universe. The one above the physical is what we normally call the emotional realm because on an individual level it corresponds to your emotional body or mind. On the collective level it corresponds to the emotional body of humankind as a whole. Above this is what we call the mental realm or the realm of thought. Above that is the highest vibration of the material world, which is the level where your identity is defined.

If you look back at history, you will see that humankind has actually been going through a progressive stage, a progressive process of initiations. If you go far enough back, you see that human beings were focused at the physical level, dealing with their physical environment, struggling against the physical environment. They were focused at the level of action. Actually, Moses and the exodus from Egypt could be seen as a way for the people to rise above this level.

The next level up is the emotions. When you have gained some awareness and control over your actions, you will begin to work more on your emotions. You become more aware of how the emotions control your actions. You see the need to control your emotions if you are to truly control your actions. I have said that in order to follow my command to turn the other cheek, you have to be able to control your reactions to other people. If you are to avoid either fleeing or fighting back, then you need to be in command of your emotions, or they will take over your mind and you will act without being able to stop the action.

In order to control your emotions, you need to have control over your thoughts. Your thoughts define the parameters for how you react to situations and what emotions you consider acceptable. At an even deeper level, you need to realize that your thoughts are defined within the framework set by your sense of identity. If, for example, you see yourself as a miserable sinner who was created in sin and who by nature is prone to sin, then there are certain thoughts you simply cannot accept. There are certain feelings you cannot cultivate, there are certain feelings you cannot avoid when you believe yourself to be a miserable sinner who has no value.

The forces of anti-christ at the physical level

There are four levels of the material universe. At the physical level you find people who are in physical embodiment and who have embodied the consciousness of anti-christ to a very high degree. They are almost completely blinded by the consciousness of anti-christ. This means that they can always justify their actions, and they believe their actions can be justified by some higher goal. The ends can justify the means.

As an obvious example of this, take Adolf Hitler who believed that the higher goal he had defined justified the killing of all Jews on this planet. Take Stalin in Russia who believed that the goal of promoting communism and keeping himself in power justified the killing of millions of his own people. Mao Zedong in China had the exact same attitude and killed even more of his own people than Stalin. These are obvious examples from history. You can also find certain serial killers or serial rapists who have the same attitude.

Nevertheless, be not fooled into thinking that only people who are recognized as having done something evil have embodied the consciousness of anti-christ. There are many who have not been recognized because they have been so good at disguising themselves that they are not seen as oppressors but in some cases even as the saviors or the leaders of the people. You have many big industrialists who felt completely superior to the workers they employed and who simply gathered riches and power for themselves regardless of the consequences for the people or for the society in which they lived. You have many other people who on a smaller scale have been completely blinded by the illusion that working for some superior cause justified that they forced other people.

Can you begin to see that even some of the leaders of Christian churches fall into this category, both in the past and today? I can assure you that the majority of the Popes of the Catholic Church have been fallen beings in embodiment who have been blinded by the consciousness of anti-christ. Surely, they have believed that they were working for the cause of Christ, but as I have said many times, if you commit violence and force others, if you violate the Law of Free Will, you cannot be working for Christ.

There are people in physical embodiment who are so blinded by anti-christ that they will do certain things to kill the Living Christ either physically or at least psychologically or spiritually. Many of these people have been in leadership positions and have used their positions in very subtle ways to discourage any among the general population from claiming any sort of ability or knowledge beyond what was accepted by the collective consciousness.

Look at how many people have taken a stand for something, for some new idea, and have been persecuted by the establishment or even by the general population who were also blinded by the standard of perfection promoted by their leaders. Look at how many of the inventors, writers, artists, philosophers and thinkers of history have at first been persecuted or in other ways discouraged from developing their talents or from expressing them in a public setting.

Where do you think humankind would have been today if there had not been this power elite who discouraged innovation and new thinking? I can assure you that society would have been at a much higher level than it is today. Surely, within the last one hundred to two hundred years the power elite has lost some of its ability to hold back innovation. Yet they have lost this ability primarily in the area of science and technology, but they have not lost it in other areas. In fact, they have strengthened their ability to hold back ideas in the areas of religion, spirituality, philosophy and political thinking. Here they have managed to clamp down on the academic and educational communities so that they have become extremely efficient suppression mechanisms that suppress any dangerous or unusual ideas, the very ideas that could bring society forward.

The forces of anti-christ at the emotional level

Let us now look at the emotional realm. There is an energy field around the physical planet and around your physical body. Part of that energy field is what we call the emotional realm. When you look at history, it should not be difficult to see that humankind collectively has produced an enormous amount of emotional energy that is charged with the lower emotions. These emotions all spring from fear, the fear that is inherent in the consciousness of separation.

Once you have some connection to oneness, you know that there is a part of you that can never actually die. The Conscious You is an extension of the Creator's Being and cannot die. When you step into the consciousness of separation and begin to see yourself as a separate being, it is inevitable that you will fear that you can die. Truly, the separate being, the separate self, *can* die; it is mortal, but the Conscious You cannot. As long as the Conscious You identifies itself with the separate self, the Conscious You believes that it can die and that it *will* die when the separate self dies, or even when the physical body dies. The basic feeling is fear, and from that springs all of the other lower feelings: anger, hatred, jealousy, whatever you have.

When you look at humankind and the amount of conflicts even in known history, you will see that an enormous amount of energy has been produced that has taken on the vibrations of these lower feelings. Science has told you that energy cannot be created or destroyed. This is a truth with modifications, but it is correct that once energy has taken on a certain vibration, it will remain in that vibration until some external force acts upon it and either reduces its vibration further or raises its vibration again.

This is why it is possible for the inhabitants of earth to create such a concentration of fear-based energy that the energy actually starts forming something that is similar to a maelstrom, a tornado or a black hole. The energy starts swirling and moving, and it exerts a magnetic pull on the emotional bodies of human beings. That is why it is entirely possible that a human being can be overwhelmed by the emotional energies in the collective consciousness.

You might recall that there is a situation in the scriptures where an angry mob was ready to stone a woman caught in adultery. I went up against that mob, and I was able to help them snap out of the mob consciousness. What had actually happened was that a number of individuals had already, on an individual basis, opened up their emotional bodies to the energies of the collective. When these individuals came together in condemnation of this woman, they all lost their ability to act as individuals and now they acted with a mob mind.

You see many examples of this throughout history. You see, for example, that almost the entire German population, during the years before and during the Second World War, were overpowered by a collective emotional downward spiral that made them susceptible to the manipulations of Hitler and the forces behind him.

In the case of the woman caught in adultery, I was able to help the people snap out of the mob consciousness so that they could walk away as individuals. As you see in my arrest, trial and crucifixion, I was not always able to do this, for again free will reigns supreme. The Christ cannot act against people's free will if they are not willing to let the Christ take them out of their current state of consciousness so they can see beyond the perception filter that blinds them.

You need to recognize that there are very strong forces, very strong vortexes of fear-based energy, in the collective consciousness of earth. Many of the people that you see committing crimes or other atrocities are overpowered by such a vortex and they lose control of their actions. As a Christed being or a person striving for Christhood, you need to become very aware of this, and you need to take practical steps and use the tools we have defined in order to free yourself from the downward pull of this emotional energy.

The forces of anti-christ at the mental level

When you go to the mental level, there are again certain patterns or vortexes that have been created by thought energy. You will, for example, in today's world see that there has been created a very powerful vortex of intellectual energy based on a denial of God, a denial of a spiritual side to life. This vortex has become so strong that many people find that their individual minds have been overpowered by this vortex so that they are no longer actually thinking as individuals. They are simply following the currents in the collective consciousness.

They will claim that they are free thinkers because they reject religion and religious programming, but they have simply stepped into another vortex of programming. It is perfectly true that the Christian religion did form a very powerful vortex in the mental body of earth and that it was extremely strong during the Middle Ages. It had a very powerful influence on peoples' minds and ability to think, and it was truly responsible for creating the Dark Ages where there was not the innovation that could have brought society forward.

If you really are a free thinker in this age, it is necessary to free your mind from the vortex, from the programming, created by Christianity over these past almost 2,000 years. It is equally important to free your mind from the vortex of materialism created over the last several hundred years. If you step from one vortex into another, you have not actually become a free thinker; you have not actually made progress. The ultimate way to become a free thinker is to reach for the consciousness of

Christ. It is the *only* way to free yourself from the collective vortexes of ideas or thinking that envelop this planet as a dense cloud.

The forces of anti-christ at the identity level

When you go to the identity level, there are very strong vortexes that define who you are as a human being. The Christian religion has created the vortex that you are a sinner by nature, that you were created flawed and imperfect. This is not correct when you talk about your true identity, what I have called the Conscious You. It is, however, correct when you talk about the separate self, the self that is defined based on the consciousness of anti-christ.

Can you see how the fallen beings, the blind leaders, have created a double deception? What is flawed, what was created in sin, was the separate self. They have created the vortex of energy in the identity body of the planet which says this is all there is to you. There is no part of your identity, no part of your being, that is beyond this. They have taken a truth and turned it into an untruth.

In rebellion against this flawed vortex of identity, another group of fallen beings, of false leaders, have created the philosophy that you are not even a sinner created by God for there is no God. You are a product of a mindless process of evolution, you are a more sophisticated ape, a hairless ape, and there is nothing spiritual to your identity. In fact, your identity is an illusion for all of your mental, emotional and psychic processes are products of chemical reactions, material reactions, in the physical brain.

These are two forms of denial of the reality of who you are, namely a spiritual being with a Christ potential. Both of them are created by a power elite that wants to shut Christ out of this world by getting you to voluntarily deny the Christ in yourself.

The only way the Christ can enter this world is through an individual human being. The ultimate way to shut Christ out is to get all people to deny their Christ potential, thereby denying the universal Christ mind the opportunity to express itself through their individual minds.

Disembodied forces of anti-christ

What needs to be added to this picture is that as there are human beings in a physical body who have embodied the consciousness of anti-christ to a high degree, there are also beings in the other three realms that have embodied this consciousness. In the modern world the materialists have scoffed at any possibility that there is something beyond the material world. They have ridiculed the medieval beliefs in demons or various mythological creatures.

If you look at all of the myths of the world, all of the creatures that are talked about do in fact exist, only they do not exist in the material realm. They exist, most of them, in the emotional realm. These myths did not come out of peoples' imagination in the sense that they just made them up. In most cases, people actually had visions of the emotional realm and saw the creatures that exist there and that are manifestations of the fear-based emotions.

What you need to realize beyond this is that in the emotional realm are beings who have embodied the consciousness of anti-christ to such a degree that they are not actually allowed to take physical embodiment. You need to understand why this is so.

Once you are in a physical body, you have the capacity to physically harm another human being; you can go and kill that person physically. If a being has embodied the consciousness of anti-christ to a critical degree, it will not be allowed to take physical embodiment on earth, but it can still be allowed to exist in the emotional realm. From this realm, such a being can still seek to influence people, but it cannot physically force them under its influence. They must *choose* to allow this being to influence their emotional bodies. This is a choice that must be made.

Many people in embodiment are not aware that they have made this choice because it was made long time ago in the past, in a past lifetime long forgotten. That is why you see many people on earth who have such big holes in their emotional bodies that they are almost like robots who are controlled by the beings in the emotional realm. Why do you think, for example, that almost every police department on this planet experiences an increase in crime or violence around the time of the full moon? It is simply because of the influence from the emotional realm that overpowers the emotions of some people and therefore causes them to commit acts of violence or crime.

There are people who are permanently overpowered by these beings in the emotional realm and have very little control over their actions. They are the ones you see commit crimes or atrocities, such as killing or torturing others. As I am speaking these words, there has for several years been a civil war going on in Syria and there are many reports of torture, even of children being tortured in front of their parents. How do you think it is possible for a human being to torture a child? It is not possible unless that person has lost all control of its mind and it has been taken over by beings in the emotional or even in the mental realm.

How dark beings steal your life energy

What you find in the emotional realm are beings who are what you would call evil. They have an evil intent to destroy, to force, to overpower human beings in embodiment. Why do they do this? Because these beings have cut themselves off from receiving life-giving spiritual energy directly from the spiritual realm.

One aspect of the scientific understanding that everything is energy is precisely that the material universe is created from energy from a higher realm that has been reduced in vibration. This is even embodied in Einstein's famous formula, $E = mc^2$.

Nothing can actually exist in the material world if it was not for a stream of energy from the spiritual realm that is constantly upholding the material world. When you go into the consciousness of anti-christ and start violating other people, you will gradually cut yourself off from this stream of energy. You will not be able to receive it, yet no being can exist without energy. If you cannot receive it from the spiritual realm, you must take it from one of the realms of the material world.

The beings who are confined to the emotional realm must take energy from the emotional level, and they do this by overpowering the emotions of individuals in physical embodiment and getting them to take actions that generate negative emotional energy. The beings in the emotional realm can now absorb this energy and use it to sustain themselves, possibly even to expand their powers.

They look at human beings as simply cows that are milked for their energy. They get people, on a regular basis, to engage in negative feelings and negative actions. Thereby, people produce the energy that feeds these beings in the emotional realm, these fallen beings. There are beings in the emotional realm who are what you would traditionally see as the devil or as the demons of hell. They are obviously evil, they are obviously aggressive, and they are seeking to destroy people and stir up conflict and unrest.

Christian leaders overpowered by demons

It is an absolute truth that during the history of the Christian religion, many Christians, even many Christian leaders, have been overpowered by these fallen beings in the emotional realm. That is why it has been possible for Christians to engage in violence, from the massacre of the Cathars to the inquisition, the witch hunts, the crusades, the persecution of scientists, the wars between Catholics and Protestants, going all the way up to modern times.

Even today, many Christians are overpowered by these destructive beings in the emotional realm. Why do you think it is possible for many Christians in the United States to feel that the invasion of Iraq was justified by God or justified by Christ, as certain prominent American Christian preachers proclaimed? It is only because their emotional bodies have been overpowered by beings in the emotional realm. They stirred up people's emotions to the point where they felt it was necessary, even justified, to use violence to spread Christianity throughout the world.

It is astounding to me that there are still people in today's age who can feel this way. It is astounding to me that there are people who will follow these blind leaders in the Christian churches who proclaim that violence is justified in the name of Christ. Where is your hearts, your Christ discernment, your ability to know what is love and what is anti-love?

There is only one explanation for any Christian feeling that violence is justified. That person has been overpowered by the fallen beings, the demonic beings, in the emotional realm. There is *no other way* that you can take the step of committing violent actions and thinking this is justified in the name of Christ.

The wolves in sheep's clothing

Beyond the beings in the emotional realm, who are what you would call obviously dark or evil, there is another class of fallen beings who exist in the mental and the identity realms. These are beings who are not normally seen as dark or evil for they are so good at disguising themselves.

They are the ones who have created these elaborate thought systems, ideologies, belief systems that define truth. They have set themselves up as the gods who appear benign, who appear to have authority, who appear to be so smart. They *are* smart compared to many human beings, but they are smart only in the way that they have developed their ability to use the consciousness of anti-christ to argue for the ideas that they are using to manipulate human beings.

These are truly the false preachers. Many preachers in physical embodiment have been overpowered, have had their mental and identity bodies overpowered, by fallen beings in the identity and mental realms. Some people in physical embodiment have embodied this consciousness of using the mind of anti-christ to argue *against* the existence of God or to argue *for* the existence of a false god.

It will be uncomfortable for many people to realize that the history of religion on this planet has been strongly influenced by these fallen beings in the identity realm, in the mental realm and in physical embodiment. They are the ones who have perverted religions and turned them into systems for justifying violence. *There is no other explanation for the fact that religion has been used to justify violence.*

12 | HOW TO FREE CHRISTIANITY FROM ANTI-CHRIST

Why am I giving you these teachings about the forces of anti-christ? My goal for this book is to give teachings so that those who have ears to hear and eyes to see can recreate Christianity as a religion that actually teaches the true teachings of Christ rather than the teachings of anti-christ. How can you free the Christian religion and your own view of the Christian religion from the consciousness of anti-christ unless you realize what the consciousness of anti-christ is, and that there are forces who are doing everything they can to keep you and every other human being blinded by, entrapped by, the consciousness of anti-christ?

I came 2,000 years ago to set the captives free. Free from what? Free from the power elite whose members have embodied the consciousness of anti-christ to a very high degree and who are using it to enslave the majority of the people on earth. How will you be free unless you wisen up, unless you become as I said: "Wise as serpents and harmless as doves?" The first step is to become completely and utterly non-violent because you will never free yourself from the power elite by fighting the power elite.

This is a trap set by the power elite, set by the false teachers of this planet, the fallen beings on this planet.

Violence is never justified by God

There are forces in the emotional realm who are completely focused on themselves and focused on manipulating and even destroying human beings in order to milk them of their energy. These are the forces who use open violence and open force. They seek to take over human beings in embodiment and get them to use violence and force against others. These are forces that are completely controlled by their selfish desires, by their very short-term selfish desires.

What you need to recognize is that there are those in the mental and identity realms who are actually using the forces in the emotional realm to keep people trapped in the duality consciousness. They have done this by creating various thought systems that say it is justified by God, it is necessary for the fulfillment of God's plan, that you use violence to destroy the forces who are openly evil.

These are the ones who create the division that some people are working for an evil religion, an evil empire or an evil ideology. It is justified that the "good" people seek to force the other people into compliance, or even kill them if they will not comply.

You cannot become truly harmless as a dove unless you see through the illusions used by the serpents, those who have embodied the consciousness of anti-christ and become so sophisticated that they can use it to argue for or against absolutely anything, absolutely any idea expressed on earth.

Thesis, anti-thesis and synthesis

There is a philosopher, named Hegel, who came up with the observation that there are certain forces that shape the evolution of this world. The common interpretation of this is that any idea forms a thesis but it creates its own anti-thesis. The interaction between thesis and anti-thesis creates a new idea, namely a synthesis. There is truth to this observation but what you need to add is the consciousness of anti-christ.

As I have explained, the consciousness of anti-christ is separated from oneness, which means that it must have at least two divisions. Furthermore, the divisions in the consciousness of anti-christ cannot be complementary forces; they must – by their very nature and the very nature of anti-christ – be opposing forces.

If you have a force, an idea or a thought system that is based on the consciousness of anti-christ, it will have an opposite. It will feel threatened by the opposite, which means it cannot peacefully co-exist with the opposite. It must oppose it and seek to destroy it. Those who are not wise as the serpent, and even the serpents themselves, do not realize that one of the opposing forces that spring from anti-christ can never destroy the other. The two polarities of anti-christ appear at the same time, they appear only in relation to each other. They are defined in opposition to each other and they can only exist in relation to each other.

If you managed to destroy one polarity, you would at the same time destroy the other. You cannot actually destroy any of them. You might suppress one and make the other superior in power for a time, but this can only last for a time. Anything you do from the consciousness of anti-christ has an opposite reaction, also from the consciousness of anti-christ, and the two will eventually break down each other. What you need to do is become wise as serpents so you realize that it is not a matter of destroying one and elevating the other, it is a matter of transcending *both* aspects of the consciousness of anti-christ.

How Christ makes progress possible

If both the thesis and the anti-thesis are defined by the consciousness of anti-christ where do you think the synthesis will take you? It will take you further into the quicksand of anti-christ. Why has it been possible for humankind to progress rather than going into a self-destructive spiral, as past civilizations have actually done? It is because there has been a small number of people who have been willing to be the open doors for the consciousness of Christ to be expressed in this world. The only thing that can drive progress and prevent a self-destructive, downward spiral is that more and more people begin to embody the consciousness of Christ so that they become the open doors for the universal Christ consciousness to express itself through their individual minds.

This is what I came to illustrate as an example for all to follow. Here is what you need to understand if you are to free the Christian religion from the consciousness of anti-christ. The Christ works in two ways. There are some people who are able to encounter the Living Christ and to allow the Living Christ to take them out of their perception filter so they have a mystical experience of a higher state of consciousness, pure awareness, the flowing spirit, the Holy Spirit, and Christ Truth. There are those who are not ready for this experience so the Living Christ must give them a teaching expressed in words.

What most Christians today would like to believe is that when I walked the earth 2,000 years ago, I gave a complete and perfect teaching expressed in words that will stand for all time. This simply is not possible and here is one of the main reasons why it is not possible. Once the Living Christ appears and gives a teaching expressed in words, the people who are overshadowed by the forces of anti-christ will immediately begin perverting that teaching. In the beginning, there are certain forces of anti-christ who will seek to destroy the person who is the open door, as they killed my physical body. Then, they will seek to use violence to suppress or persecute the followers of the Living Christ.

If this is not successful, or if they cannot get the majority of the people to simply ignore the expression of the Living Christ, then they will join the movement. Now they will use the consciousness of anti-christ to interpret, or rather *dis*-interpret, the words given by the Living Christ so that they become turned into a polarity that springs from the mind of anti-christ. There will be other representatives of the forces of anti-christ who will create an opposite to the first interpretation. Now you have the emergence of two opposing interpretations of the words and the teachings of the Living Christ, and these will be in opposition to each other.

How Constantine perverted Christianity

If you will study the history of the Christian religion, you will see the seeds of this in the first couple of centuries, but it really becomes obvious after the formation of the Roman Catholic Church. The Emperor Constantine elevated Christianity to the status of the Roman State religion because he hoped it would unify his empire under his command. No sooner had he done so than he realized that the Christian religion was divided into two opposing camps. The topic that divided them was the nature of Christ. Was I of a fundamentally different nature than all other human beings, or was I of the same nature as human beings but had reached a higher level of spiritual development? You can go back and see this as what is known as the Arian controversy that divided the Church into an Eastern and a Western branch. The Western branch was controlled by the Roman Catholic Church until the Reformation of Luther. If you are to free the Christian religion from this influence of the consciousness of anti-christ, you need to be willing to look at the history of the Christian religion and see how – from a very early stage, even from the presence of Peter as the disciple who would not surrender into oneness with me – it was influenced by the consciousness of anti-christ. You need to see how this consciousness created certain interpretations that have an opposite and therefore create a conflict and division in the church.

If you look at the Arian controversy, you need to see that it is not a matter of "was the one side right and the other side wrong?" Both of them had certain elements that cannot be said to be directly wrong, but these elements were put into a context that made them wrong, that destroyed the example of Christ and the path of Christ. You need to be willing to go through the history of Christianity and see these fallacies. Then you need to develop your inner attunement with my Living Presence so that you can receive from within the reality of Christ that helps you rise above both of the dualistic, relative, serpentine interpretations.

Jesus never defined a church or a pope

I have said before that you cannot know Christ through a mental image but only through a direct experience. Take the very concept that an outer church represents Christ. This is the claim made by the Roman Catholic Church, namely that it is the only true representative of Christ on earth because it has the authority going back to Peter as the first Pope. Well, I never defined a church that is anything like the Roman Catholic Church. I never appointed Peter as the first Pope of that church or any other church. I never defined a clear organizational structure or doctrine or set up scriptures, rules or rituals.

I left the Christian movement to be guided by the Holy Spirit, by the Comforter, not by outer rules and doctrines. What the consciousness of anti-christ does as its first order of business is to undermine the belief in, and the willingness to be the open door for, the spirit. It comes in and says: "We cannot have this chaos of all these people speaking by the spirit; we need to have a uniform organizational structure and doctrine so that people know what a Christian church is and know what to expect. We need to define the Christian religion so that it sets itself apart from other religions, otherwise how can we claim that the Christian religion is the only true religion and the others are false?"

Who says you have to claim that there is only one true religion and that the others are false? I know Christians will refer to certain statements of mine about making all people into my disciples and about no one coming to the Father save through me, but the real road to the Father is the universal Christ consciousness. You do not attain the Christ consciousness through me; you attain it by finding it in the kingdom of God within you so that you become an open door for the Christ consciousness. *That* is the only road to the Father.

A movement guided by the Holy Spirit

What I wanted the Christian movement to do was to preach that message and to give people both the outer and the inner path, the lower and the higher path, whereby they could raise their consciousness until every human being becomes an open door for the Living Christ.

You do not need to worry about whether people are saying different things in different contexts. It is true that there are false spirits. There are false spirits in the emotional, in the mental and in the identity realm. When I left my disciples, there were some of them who had the ability to be the open door for the Holy Spirit and let the Holy Spirit speak through them. There were others who had not raised their consciousness to that level. They had their consciousness attuned to either the emotional, the mental or the lower identity realms and so they were open doors for spirits from those realms.

It is perfectly true that there was a somewhat disconnected message given, but nevertheless there was still the openness that some people could be a true open door for the one, unified, Holy Spirit. This was better than what happened later when the Christian movement completely shut the door for this possibility. It is better that people are the open doors for a lower spirit because it still gives them the opportunity to raise their discernment and eventually come to see through the divisions of the lower spirits and therefore reach for the one Holy Spirit.

Even if people are open doors for the Holy Spirit, it does not mean they will always say the same message. The Living Christ comes to a specific group of people at a specific level of consciousness and it gives them a teaching that is meant to raise them one step higher. The Christ may indeed adapt its message to the beliefs and the cultural context in which it appears, and therefore it may say something to one group of people that may appear – from the interpretation of the linear mind – to be in opposition to what is said to another group of people.

This is a distinct possibility because so many people on earth are so trapped in so many serpentine illusions that you cannot give them the strong meat of the pure teaching of Christ. You need to give them what they can grasp and what will take them one step higher—and then you can give them a higher teaching. What those in the serpentine mind will do is that they will look at a worded expression and they will interpret it literally. Then they will take another worded expression and interpret *that* literally and say: "But these two oppose each other and therefore they cannot both be true. We must determine which one is true and which one is false; and in order to determine this we must create a definition of perfection for what the Christian religion is all about and what the true interpretation of the words of Christ is."

With all I have told you in this book, can you begin to see that any time you create this standard of perfection – and say that this is the *only* true way to interpret the teachings of Christ – you have actually lost the Spirit of Christ? You have created a mental image, a graven image, a representation of Christ. You are looking at Christ from a distance. You are looking at Christ through the filter of your graven image. You are wanting Christ to conform to your image rather than grasping for the Living Spirit that can take you beyond your mental box. This is the opposite of what Christ wants for you.

No church can fully represent Christ

There is no church on earth that ever has or ever will be a true representative of Christ. The Christ does not want a *representation* on earth for any representation will be based on a mental image created by the consciousness of anti-christ. It does not matter what it says, it will still be based on anti-christ. The only way to know Christ is through the direct inner experience that is beyond words. A true Christian movement will teach people this, will teach people the necessity of reaching beyond words for the direct experience. You do not need a *representation* of Christ when you have the direct *experience*.

There are those who are not ready for the direct experience, and they do need a worded teaching and an organizational structure that tells them about the lower path of Christ. Do you see that the official Christian religion is not such an organization because it does not teach you about a path? It does not teach you about the necessity to reach beyond the words for the direct experience. It does not teach that if you keep following the path, you will come to the point where you will have this experience and that this is the true purpose of Christianity, of being a Christian.

What the official churches started doing at a fairly early stage was that they started defining themselves as the only true path to salvation. The very moment you make the claim to exclusivity, you have demonstrated – clearly and undeniably – that you have been completely blinded by the consciousness of anti-christ. Only the consciousness of anti-christ will make this claim about an outer organization or an outer worded statement or teaching. Only the consciousness of anti-christ can claim that it is possible to represent Christ in this world.

The scribes and Pharisees of Christianity

A true Christian movement always points beyond to the direct experience. It is really quite simple when you snap out of the subtle serpentine lies that have infused the Christian religion for seventeen hundred years and more. If you look at some of the discussions that have taken place between some of the prominent theologians of the Christian religion, you will see an immense amount of clever intellectual reasoning. Almost from the very beginning, there were people in the Christian movement who were very much taken over by beings in the mental realm. They could therefore give expression to these very clever intellectual arguments that seemingly proves absolutely any point with ultimate authority.

Why do you think I opposed the scribes and the Pharisees who were the intellectuals of the Jewish religion? Because I did not come to save these people. Nothing can save them, given the Law of Free Will. I came for those who are meek, which means they are willing to realize that their minds have a limitation and that they need to reach for the direct experience of a higher level of consciousness than both the mental and the lower identity realm. They need to reach beyond the power elite who are dominated by these realms, by the serpentine mind, by the consciousness of anti-christ. They need to free their minds from the influence, from the ideologies, from the interpretations and the mental images created by the blind leaders, the false teachers in the mental and identity realms.

These beings are very, very clever. They are so clever that even I, when I was in physical embodiment, could not come up with an argument that would convince them. Once you decide that "this is a truth that cannot be questioned," there is no argument made with words that will prove undeniably the fallacy of your belief. You will always be able to come up with an argument with words that counteracts any other argument made with words. There are beings in the mental and identity realms who have been playing this game for much longer than most people are willing to believe.

They have not tired of it. The real question is: "Have *you* tired of it?" I tell you that I had enough of it, and that is why I did not engage them on *their* terms but simply attempted to confound their minds with these abrupt statements meant to confuse the analytical, linear mind. Because I had had enough of this and did not engage them, I qualified for my ascension. Had I gone into a mental battle with these people, I would not have fulfilled my mission and qualified for my ascension.

I could potentially still be arguing with these very same people, most of whom are still in embodiment and still sitting in their institutions of intellectualism. Many of them are now in the area of science and education, but some are still in theological circles. They are still arguing the same old tired arguments that lead absolutely nowhere, meaning they never lead to a fundamentally higher state of consciousness. These people have been going around in circles for thousands upon thousands of years and the question is: "How long will *you* want to be on this merry-go-round that they have created?"

You are a formless spirit

If you have had enough, then I have given you the teachings and the tools for how to reach for the mind of Christ and experience a higher reality, rather than continuing to relate to that reality through mental images. You will never know God through a mental image; you will never know Christ through a mental image.

No matter how sophisticated that image might be – and no matter what claims it makes to some ultimate, infallible authority – you will know Christ and God only by rising beyond the mental mind, by rising beyond the identity mind, and realizing that you are a formless spirit.

As such, you have the capacity to experience a formless state of consciousness. Once you experience the formlessness of the Christ mind, you will experience the fallacy of all of the dualistic expressions of the mind of anti-christ.

This is such a freedom that it cannot be described in words. What I *can* do with words is to say that the potential exists. If you have already had glimpses of this experience, you need to hold on to them and seek to have more experiences. You need to clear your mind of the misqualified lower energies and the dualistic beliefs that prevent you from having these clear mystical experiences of oneness. As you engage in this path, using the tools and the teachings we have given in abundance, you can come to the point where you no longer need a mental image in order to relate to Christ, in order to relate to God or in order to relate to life in the material world.

That is when you know you have taken an important step towards freeing yourself from the downward pull of the collective consciousness and the forces of anti-christ who are doing everything they can to keep you attached to this world. What they want is to make you feel that there is still something in this world you have to do – something you have to experience, some problem you have to solve, some cause you have to fight for, some ultimate result that must be achieved – before you can leave. They want you to think that there is something unresolved that prevents you from simply leaving this world behind.

Christianity as a false path to salvation

The trick of the consciousness of anti-christ is to create two opposing polarities, to create a tension between them and then to say that there must be some ultimate outcome, some ultimate solution to this tension. Then, it projects that it is *your* job to bring about that ultimate outcome.

This is what they have done to the Christian religion. They have portrayed the Christian religion as the only path to salvation. They have projected that God wants all human beings on earth to be saved and that this can happen only if they become members of the outer Christian religion. Only when this goal has been achieved, can you be free.

I may sound as if I am not in approval of most Christians. In reality, I have a great love for all Christians and I see that many Christians have made great progress on the path towards a higher state of consciousness. Many have become almost completely non-violent, at least when it comes to outer actions.

I see that many Christians are close to taking the step to a higher level, but I also see that there is something that is preventing them from taking that step. There is something that is preventing them from acknowledging their Christ potential, and in most cases it is precisely this very clever reasoning, which comes in many disguises, that as a Christian, as a Christian minister, as a Christian leader you must get as many people as possible to join an outer Christian religion, preferably your own.

The denial of the Path of Oneness

The consciousness of anti-christ can only be based on division, not only division but opposing polarities. Anytime you set yourself apart from other people, you are trapped in the consciousness of anti-christ. There can be no other explanation. The path of Christhood leads towards oneness, which has an Alpha and an Omega aspect. The Alpha is what I exemplified when I declared: "I and my Father are one." You are walking towards a sense of oneness with the universal Christ consciousness, with the individual Christ consciousness for you, with your own higher being and spiritual self—and with the beings in the spiritual realm who are your spiritual parents.

You are also walking a path towards oneness with all people here below, oneness with all life. I exemplified this when I said: "Inasmuch as ye have done it unto the least of these my brethren, ye have done it unto me." I knew I was one with all people and I knew that whatever was done by the consciousness of anti-christ to any person on earth was done to me.

Can you see that by defining the Christian religion as the only true road to salvation, the forces of anti-christ have instantaneously created a division between Christians and non-Christians? As a Christian, you feel it is your duty to convert all other people to the outer religion of Christianity. You think that this outer religion is the road to salvation. The outer religion is *not* the road to salvation; it is the Christ consciousness.

This is the message that I wanted preached to every creature, this is the message that is the only doorway to the kingdom of God. It is this message that the true Christian movement will preach. Any Christian church that preaches a different message, a message that denies the path and the Christ potential, is taken over by the consciousness of anti-christ.

12 | How to Free Christianity from Anti-Christ

The potential for a renewal of Christianity

I see the potential that many people in the Christian movement would snap out of this spiritual blindness, this spiritual pride and arrogance, and instantly have the scales fall from their eyes, as it happened to Paul on the road to Damascus. What happened to Paul was that he had accepted a perception filter whereby he looked at Jesus Christ through the filter of anti-christ. When he encountered my Living Presence, he was willing to look at the beam in his own eye, to recognize that he had elements of anti-christ in his being and to accept the Living Presence of Christ instead. That is why the scales fell from his eyes; because of his willingness to re-examine his beliefs.

What I am telling you here is that there are two polarities in the consciousness of anti-christ. One polarity makes you *deny* Christ, which is what happened to Paul. The other makes you *accept* Christ, but you are not accepting the Living Spirit of Christ, you are accepting a mental image of Christ created by the consciousness of anti-christ.

You think you are *accepting* Christ, but you are *denying* Christ. You are accepting a false Christ, a false spirit and denying the Living Spirit that I am. This you can snap out of in an instant. Some will be ready to snap out of it instantly, others will not be ready and need to follow a path before they can have the scales fall from their eyes.

That is why I have given this book and many other teachings and tools through this messenger and other sources. The tools and the teachings are in the physical realm where anyone who is willing can find them and apply them. They can therefore purify their consciousness of the elements of anti-christ until they are ready for the direct encounter with the Living Spirit of Christ—on the road to Damascus or wherever you think you are heading, based on the illusions of anti-christ that make you think you have to fulfill a certain goal.

Paul was on the road. He had a goal. He thought it was a superior goal. He was willing to let the Living Christ blind him with the truth so that he could no longer see the dualistic divisions of anti-christ. He saw only the blinding, unified light of Christ. He was willing to change course, to change the course of his life and say: "No more will I persecute those who are following Jesus Christ. I will instead strive to walk the path that he outlined so that I can come to the point where I have let the mind of Christ be in me. I have let that mind be in me which was also in Christ Jesus, and therefore I have fulfilled my Christ potential and claimed my identity as a Son or Daughter of God."

Many in the Christian movement, both leaders and ordinary members, are ready to make that quantum leap in consciousness. They are ready to consciously acknowledge that they have been following a false path, disguised as the only true path of Christ. They are ready to step up and consciously acknowledge that there must be more to Christianity, there must be more to the true teachings of Christ, than what they have been given, what they have been handed down from the churches.

An incredible opportunity in this age

These churches have now, for almost 2,000 years, let thesis be opposed by anti-thesis and create a synthesis that took them further into the quagmire of anti-christ. Then, that synthesis became a new thesis that created its own anti-thesis and created a new synthesis that was even further into the jungle of anti-christ.

This has been going on now for almost 2,000 years. When will *you* have had enough? I tell you that I, the Living Christ, had enough a very long time ago. I know I said: "In your patience possess ye your soul," and it does apply in certain instances. But it does not apply if it keeps you trapped in the consciousness of anti-christ indefinitely. There must come a point where you make a decisive decision and say: "No more! It is time to know the true path and the true Spirit of Christ, and this is what I want for my life. I no longer want a substitute. I want the real, Living Spirit."

Ask and ye shall receive. Ask with an open mind and heart and you shall receive the inner experience that is beyond the doubts of the serpents. If you are not ready for the inner experience, then follow the outer path. Study the teachings, apply the tools and you *will* become ready. I will appear to you in a blinding light so that the scales will fall from your eyes and you will see the true path of Christ. Not the path that I taught 2,000 years ago, but the path that I teach today. The collective consciousness has been raised, and you can go much further on the path today than people could back then. You can do greater works than I did because we have entered a new cycle and we have raised the collective consciousness to new heights.

You are facing an incredible opportunity in this age. You may look back at the time 2,000 years ago when I walked the earth in a physical body. You may see that I came in contact with many people, actually thousands of people. You may see that many of them might have been moved, might have been healed, but after I was no longer physically there, they went back to their ordinary lives. There were only a relative few, more than my disciples but still only a relative few, who actually followed me and radically changed their lifestyle.

You may look at the many people who met me and who did not change, and you may see that they lost an opportunity that was unique because I was there in a physical body. I tell you, I am here today in my spiritual body. I am speaking through this messenger right now, but I can express myself through many people and have done so. I am willing to express myself through *you,* if you will give me room, if you will let there be room in the inn for the Living Christ to be born in you.

You are facing an opportunity today that is fully as great as the opportunity people faced 2,000 years ago. The difference is that I do not appear in a physical body, I appear in a form that requires a higher level of sophistication and openness of heart and mind in order to recognize me, but the opportunity is there.

Why did you embody at this time?

There has never been, in the history of the earth, a greater opportunity to walk the true path of Christ than right now in this age. There has never been a greater need for many, many people who are willing to walk that path and openly demonstrate it. If my words stir something in your heart, then acknowledge that you are one of the people who volunteered to embody at this specific time in order to consciously and openly walk the true path of Christ and demonstrate it to others. *Then get on with demonstrating it!*

You did not come here to dilly-dally in the illusions of anti-christ for almost an entire lifetime. You came here to be like Paul, to let the scales fall from your eyes and to then go out and preach the true path of Christ. Grab the opportunity, my beloved. Grab it now, or grab it when you are ready, for I am with you always even unto the end of the earth. This does not mean that the world will end; it means that the cycle will end where the forces of anti-christ are allowed to embody on this planet. That day will come, not in the near future but it will come. It will only come when a critical mass of people grab the opportunity to walk the path of Christ and embody, demonstrate and express their individual Christhood as I expressed mine 2,000 years ago.

I have played my part on the stage of earth. The Law of Free Will will not allow me to reenter a physical body. It *will* allow *you,* who are in a physical body, to manifest your Christhood. *That* is why you chose to come into embodiment at this time.

Grab the opportunity and walk the path with me. Set aside all these other things. Leave your nets and follow me, and I will make you true fishers of men who can awaken people to the reality of the inner path of Christ, not the false path defined by the false teachers, the blind leaders, but the true path from the Christ who sees all and who sees God in all.

13 | HOW GRACE AND WORKS WORK TOGETHER

I have talked about the necessity to take a critical look at the history of the Christian religion in order to see how it has been influenced by the consciousness of anti-christ. This is a big job. This is an extensive task that would require people to look at many different aspects of history. Nevertheless, I wish to give you one example of how this must be done. Consider one of the great schisms that has divided the Christian religion in the West between the Roman Catholic Church and the various Protestant denominations. This is the debate about whether you are saved through grace alone, or through grace *and* works.

When you look at the historical setting for this, you will see that the Catholic Church, up through the Middle Ages, had added many things to Christianity that clearly were not in accordance with my teachings. The most blatant of these was, of course, the letters of absolvency where you could buy the absolution of your sins. Nevertheless, there were many other things added, including a very subtle mindset of exclusivity that only Catholics would go to heaven because they followed the rules of an outer religion. This is also part of works, not only that you do good works for others in the form of charity, but that you perform good works in supporting the Church in all ways, including being obedient to church hierarchy.

It should be possible for those who have read this book to see that you do not score points with Christ by blindly following the blind leaders – the fallen beings, the false teachers – who have taken over the Catholic Church. This is not good works in the eyes of Christ. Nor is it, of course, true that you can buy your way to absolution from your sins. Nor is it, for that matter, true that an external church authority can absolve you of your sins in the first place.

I am not thereby denouncing the institution of confession. It can be helpful in a psychological sense for some people. If they can go and speak out what they have done and accept forgiveness for it, they can be helped to move on with their lives. For many people, going to confession has just become a ritual, and they go and confess some sin and then accept that they are absolved from the sin, but they do not change the consciousness that caused them to sin.

It is only the change in consciousness that I am looking for. It is only a change in consciousness that will bring you into the kingdom of God that is within you. It is only the shift from the duality consciousness, the divided consciousness, into the unified consciousness of Christ, the consciousness of oneness, that will bring you to heaven, so to speak. Heaven is a state of consciousness and that is why the kingdom of God is within you.

The fundamentalist mockery of Jesus' mission

The Catholic concept of good works was indeed very flawed. It is appropriate that Luther and other Protestant church leaders took a critical look at this. The problem was that in taking a critical look at the concept of works, they did what the duality consciousness so often makes people do. They jumped from one extreme to the other.

They reasoned that because the Catholic Church had a flawed interpretation of the concepts of works, they needed to jump to the other extreme and say that works do not contribute to your salvation for you are saved exclusively through the grace of Jesus Christ. This is what then led to the development of fundamentalist churches who say that the only thing you need to do in order to be saved is to confess Jesus Christ as your Lord and Savior.

What a complete mockery of my true mission to demonstrate the gradual path to a higher state of consciousness. What a complete and blatant disrespect for even the words of the scriptures that these fundamentalist preachers claim should be taken literally. They have made a mockery out of the scriptures by interpreting them in a way that they claim to be literal but which is anything but literal. Of course, from a logical viewpoint there can never be a literal interpretation. As soon as you are *interpreting*, you are not *literal*.

This ties in with what I have said about the consciousness of anti-christ. You see everything from a distance and therefore everything becomes a concept and every concept has an opposite and can be debated endlessly. You are now lost in the quagmire of interpretation. Do you see how this ties in with thesis versus anti-thesis, creating synthesis? The thesis was the Catholic version of works. The anti-thesis was Luther's interpretation that only grace saves you. The synthesis was the Christian fundamentalist claim that only by declaring Jesus as your Lord and Savior, will you be saved and that this is all that is needed.

Well, where is the path in Christian fundamentalist churches? It is lost, it is gone, and therefore those churches are dead to me. I can only say to them: "Get thee behind me, Satan." They have nothing whatsoever to do with my true mission.

Do I sound harsh? I do indeed intend to sound harsh for what else can cut through the veil of lies that has surrounded the people in these fundamentalist churches? They sit there every Sunday feeling holier than thou, feeling convinced that one day I will appear in the sky and give undeniable proof to all of humankind that these people in their little church somewhere were the only ones who knew the true teachings of Christ. What blatant spiritual pride and arrogance is this! How can it have anything to do with the reality of Christ? It is only and exclusively a fabrication of the mind of anti-christ and the blind leaders who have attempted to lead people astray for eons on this planet.

You need both works and grace

What is the deeper reality of works versus grace? It is that there is no works *versus* grace. It is not a matter of one or the other, *both* are necessary. You do need to perform works. Why do you need to perform works? For two reasons. One is that you need to shift your consciousness and this requires work. You need to be willing to look at the beam in your own eye, the elements of anti-christ in your own eye. You also need to transform the negative energies that have accumulated in your personal energy field, not only in this lifetime but in past lives. You also need to recognize that there is a certain reality to what Eastern religions call karma and what Christianity calls sin. In the past, you sent out an energy impulse, and this impulse will at some point be reflected back to you by the cosmic mirror of the material universe.

In the past, you have sent out these energy impulses at the level of the conscious mind and the physical body. They cycle through what I have called the four levels of the material universe, and when they come all the way back to the material realm, they manifest as various events in your life. There has been a debate, not only in Christian circles but in all religious circles, about why bad things happen to good people. Why is it that some children are born with diseases or physical handicaps or psychological handicaps? If you look only at the official Christian interpretation that reincarnation is a fallacy, then you cannot explain this.

Here is a person who has lived a good life, has gone to church every Sunday, has confessed every sin, has striven to live a life according to the outer teachings of his or her church and suddenly he or she is in a car accident and is handicapped for life. If you do not incorporate reincarnation, you cannot explain this. You can only say that this must be a good and benevolent God who wanted this to happen to that person. It must be a good and benevolent God who wanted this child to be born with a crippling disease.

Or you can come up with even more convoluted interpretations that the child must somehow have sinned, but if it was born with a disease when would it have sinned? Ah, some preachers will say, it must have sinned in the womb. Well, how exactly does a child sin in the womb? This they cannot explain for there is no logical explanation. The logical explanation is that a child sinned in a past life and is now reaping the karmic consequences of its own past choices. It was not God who wanted to punish the child, but God has given all lifestreams free will and has set up the material universe to reflect back to them, in the future, the choices they have made in the past and the energy impulses they have sent out.

Why is there a delay factor? Because it gives you the opportunity to rise above the consciousness that caused you to sin in a past life. When you do rise above the consciousness that caused you to sin, then you do not need to reap the physical consequences of your past actions.

The universe is a learning institution

The entire material universe can be looked at as a learning institution. You are here to learn who you are and what creative abilities you have. You are here to learn to express those creative abilities in a way that raises the whole. You do this by gradually putting on the Christ consciousness whereby you become more and more aware of your oneness with your source and your oneness with all life, including all other people around you. This is Christ consciousness, the awareness that all life is one. When you know that all life is one, you know that what you do to another, you are doing to yourself.

There is an even deeper truth in my statement about doing unto others. When you do something to another, your action is a reflection of your state of consciousness. Consider, for example, what it takes to kill another human being. When you are in the Christ consciousness, you could never even conceive of killing another human being. It is only the consciousness of duality, the consciousness of anti-christ, that can make you consider killing another human being. You do this because you do not see yourself as one with that other human being. If you saw that oneness, how could you kill a part of yourself?

You are in the consciousness of separation, but what must you do in order to go into that state of consciousness? You must kill a part of yourself psychologically. Before you can kill another human being, you must have killed a part of yourself. Before you can do unto others, you must have done to yourself in a psychological sense.

This means that you are now trapped in a limited sense of self, and you carry that self with you from lifetime to lifetime until you become willing to do what I told you to do. You must look at the beam in your own eye, acknowledge the elements of anti-christ and root them out of your consciousness—cleanse yourself from these elements of anti-christ.

If you are not willing to do this, then the energy impulse that you sent out when you killed the other person in a past life will eventually come back to the physical realm. It may indeed cause you to be killed either by someone else or in an accident. It may be that in the lifetimes between when you committed that act and when the karma comes back, you have changed your outer behavior. It may appear that you are now a good Christian who is living according to all the outer rules. When you are suddenly killed in an accident, people will say: "Oh, how could that possibly happen to such a good person?"

It may very well be that you have not actually changed your state of consciousness, you have not restored what you killed in yourself. You have simply taken some control over your outer behavior, but you have not taken control over your inner being. You are not free from the consciousness that caused you to sin, and that is why the karma, the energy impulse, comes back into physical manifestation.

Christ taking the sins of the world

What does it really mean that Christ takes upon himself the sins of the world? It means something quite different from how it has been interpreted by Christianity. Christ is a universal state of consciousness that is meant to restore you to oneness, no matter how far you have gone into duality and separation. When you consider that some people have had many lifetimes on this planet and when you consider how violent of a history this planet has had, you can see that it is quite possible that there are people who, over many lifetimes, have committed so many acts that are sinful that they have created a mountain of karma for themselves.

If they were to reap the physical consequences of this, they would never have a chance to progress. They would be so burdened that they could not seriously raise their consciousness.

You do see many people who are so burdened that they have no attention left over for looking at the beam in their own eye or worrying about their psychology or how to change themselves; they are fighting for physical survival. It would be almost impossible for people to make progress in consciousness if they were so burdened by the physical consequences of their past actions.

That is why the Christ can do two things. This is not done by the Christ as a universal state of consciousness but by Christ as an embodied state of consciousness. Not necessarily physical embodiment but as an ascended being who is still working with earth. I am an ascended being, an ascended master, and I have chosen to continue to work with earth as I promised to do 2,000 years ago.

This was not a given; this was a choice I made. I am not the only ascended master who is working with earth; there are many others. We all represent the Christ as embodied Christ consciousness that is specific for earth. We are all here to help you, who are our unascended brothers and sisters, walk the true path to a higher state of consciousness, the path of personal Christhood.

What we are willing to do is to take upon ourselves the burden of the energy from your past so that you can experience a temporary relief from the return current of this energy, this karma, this sin. This gives you a reprieve. This gives you an opportunity to look at your state of consciousness and to remove yourself from the state of consciousness that caused you to commit those actions in the past. If you do make use of this opportunity, we can also set aside permanently the energy so that it does not have to descend into the physical realm ever.

Many people who walk the path of Christhood will come to a point where they become aware of their responsibility. They will take upon themselves the task of transforming the energy by using spiritual tools before it becomes physical. That way we do not have to take upon ourselves the energy, but people do it for themselves, which means we are now free to help others.

Contrary to the convoluted interpretations that have followed the saying that only grace will save you, this is not a process that happened at one time. It is simply not correct that I, Jesus Christ, have taken upon myself all the sins that have been committed up until my lifetime 2,000 years ago *and* all of the sins that could possibly be committed in the future.

This would be writing humankind a blank check, saying: "You can do anything you want, you do not have to change your consciousness. Just keep sinning and then – when you are on your deathbed, as the emperor Constantine – confess Jesus Christ as your Lord and Savior and I will take upon myself all of your sins and pay your debt."

How would people learn from that? How would they get out of the state of consciousness that caused them to sin? If they do not get out of the consciousness of separation, how can they enter the consciousness of oneness that is the *only* doorway to the ascended realm, to the spiritual realm, to what most Christians call heaven?

Multiplying the talents

What I *could* do was to look at people individually and look at their works. I could give people an initial grace, an initial setting aside of their karma, so that they were not so burdened that they could not work on themselves. This was comparable to my parable about the talents where the master gave each of the three servants a different number of talents, which represents that they each had different amounts of karma.

Once that initial grace has been given, which has been given to all people on this earth as a result of my ascension, then it is all a matter of what people do with the opportunity. Do they bury their talents in the ground or do they multiply their talents by being willing to look at the beam in their own eye and sincerely reform their state of consciousness?

This is why I have talked about the importance of a path. I, Jesus Christ, or another ascended master, gives you an initial grace in the setting aside of part of your burden. Because this burden of energy is set aside, you have an opportunity to look in the mirror, to look at the beam in your own eye and to reform your consciousness, to raise your consciousness from its current level to the next level up.

When you have done that, when you have multiplied the talents, then – and *only* then – can we give you a new portion of grace. We can give you an initial portion as a grace, as a gift. We cannot give you a second portion as a grace; we can only multiply what *you* bring back to the altar by multiplying our first offering. The first offering is a grace. The second one is a multiplication of your works, of your shift in consciousness. This is how it continues on the path to personal Christhood, through an interaction between yourself and the ascended master who is your personal master and who is therefore extending grace to you.

This is the reason why it is so detrimental to people that I have been elevated as the *only* ascended being ever. Even my mother is claimed to only have been "assumed" into heaven for no one could be like me. There are *many* ascended masters. Each person has an ascended master, and it is important that people get to know their personal master and learn to attune their outer minds to the Presence of that master. This is how you can continue to multiply what you have been given so that you can continue to receive a return current and therefore you can continue your path.

13 | How Grace and Works Work Together

Why conflicts cannot be resolved

This is how grace and works work in combination. This is the higher teaching of Christ. For those who are honest, you can see how this completely goes beyond the teachings, the interpretations, that have divided Christianity for centuries. This is because the consciousness of anti-christ will always divide you into two opposing polarities. There is no resolution, there is no reconciliation between these two opposing interpretations. That is why Christianity is no closer to reconciling Protestant and Catholic churches. They never will come closer through the consciousness of anti-christ, which can only divide.

What does the consciousness of anti-christ make people think? It makes them think: "Here we have an issue, how will you solve it? Is it through one polarity, which says works and grace, or through another polarity, which says grace only?" What have you now done? You have taken a complex issue and said that there are only two ways to look at it and those two ways are in fundamental disagreement with each other. This makes you think that you have to choose one of the two ways. It also makes you think that one must be right and the other must be wrong. Surely, they cannot both be right when they are opposites.

I agree. When two viewpoints are complete opposites, they cannot both be right, but there is a different option. They could both be *wrong!* They could both be products of the consciousness of anti-christ, and this is precisely how the power elite of the false teachers have controlled humankind for eons. They pervert the debate by setting up two opposites that both spring from the consciousness of anti-christ, and then they project out that you must choose one or the other because there is no alternative.

What does the Christ mind do? It shows you that there is an alternative to the different interpretations that spring from the mind of anti-christ. You can leapfrog the interpretations. You can make a quantum leap beyond the two opposing polarities and reach for the unifying truth of the Christ mind. This requires you to have followed the path of multiplying the grace you have been extended, multiplying it by shifting your consciousness, by removing the elements of anti-christ so that you can come to actually see the higher reality of Christ. As long as you do not reform your consciousness, your conscious mind will be pulled into one of the two extremes.

Have you ever, as a child, taken a compass and a magnet and seen how, by moving the magnet closer to the compass, you can direct the compass needle to turn towards the magnet? This is an illustration of how your conscious mind, when you are a house divided against yourself, is constantly being pulled in this or that direction by the magnetic forces created by the false teachers through the consciousness of anti-christ.

There are any number of viewpoints out there in the world that form these opposing polarities that have a magnetic force. They seek to pull your mind into pointing towards one of the polarities whereby you automatically have the other end of the compass needle point towards the opposite polarity. You must accept one, and in so doing automatically reject the other, possibly even fight against the other.

That is why I said that you need to overcome the division in your own mind and attain the single-eyed vision of the Christ mind. Thereby, your conscious mind is not a compass needle but a single point, a singularity, whereby you can see oneness because your conscious mind is not pulled into all these opposite directions in the outer world.

13 | How Grace and Works Work Together

Living in the center of consciousness

So many people are living on the periphery of consciousness instead of living at the center of consciousness. When you find the kingdom of God that is within you, you find it by coming to the center where there is no extension that can be used to divide you against yourself.

This is the higher levels of the path of Christhood. The lower levels are that you are constantly seeking to reform your state of consciousness. You are multiplying what you have been given so you can rise to the next level of consciousness above the one you are at right now. When you keep doing this, then you are on the path. You are a "Follower of the Way of Christ," as some of my early followers called themselves. You may know that they did not call themselves Christians but many called themselves "Followers of the Way" because they had understood that I did not come to give them instant salvation. I came to give them a way, a systematic path, to salvation, the salvation from within.

There is some reality behind the idea of an external savior. You do need an ascended master to give you a grace in the setting aside of the burden of your personal sin, karma or energy. You cannot rise without this grace, but if you do not multiply the initial grace, then you cannot rise further. You rise both by grace and by your efforts to multiply that grace. This is the key to restoring Christianity to being the kind of movement that I intended to start 2,000 years ago, and that I did in fact start, although it did not survive for that long before some started to take it into a different direction.

14 | THE FORCE-BASED MINDSET IN CHRISTIANITY

I now wish to speak about the need to step beyond the level of violence. I have said that there is a lower path and a higher path. The lower path is where you raise your consciousness to the point where you have risen above the need or even the idea of committing violence against others. You are not seeking to take heaven by force. You have complete respect for the free will of others *and* your own free will so you will not let them force you. When you have risen to that level and become completely non-violent, then you can begin the higher path, the inner path, of seeking inner oneness with Christ.

You have heard about Christ, the redeemer. There are many popular ideas about this, but they all revolve around me being an outer force who takes away your sin. In reality, when you have raised your consciousness to a sufficient level, you can begin to attain glimpses of experiences whereby you come into an inner sense of oneness with me, or whichever ascended master is your personal master. When you come into this oneness, then you have transcended a particular element of the consciousness of anti-christ.

The ultimate resolution to the dualistic polarities of anti-christ is that in this particular topic you do not receive an outer teaching from me. You do not receive a worded message, but you come into an experience of direct oneness with my Spirit whereby your mind is free from both of the dualistic polarities. You simply transcend the level of consciousness that defined the two polarities and defined them as the perfect, the absolute, the infallible definition of good and evil, truth and untruth.

It is through inner oneness that you are ultimately redeemed from the sin of the consciousness of anti-christ. This is redemption: oneness with me or another ascended master. There is no other redemption. God has set up the universe as a schoolroom. You who are unascended must prove to the teachers above you that you have freed yourself from all elements of anti-christ, that you have left behind your nets, that you have come to the point where you can say: "What is that to me? Nothing in this outer world means more to me than my inner oneness with Jesus Christ." *This* is true redemption.

Stop seeking to change others

What will it take to begin this higher path? It will take that you overcome all tendency to use violence or force against others. You must completely stop looking at the splinter in the eyes of your brothers and sisters and focus all attention on the beam in your own eye. As long as you are concerned about changing other people, you *cannot* – you *will not* – start the higher path of Christ. That is why all of the Christians out there, all of the pastors and ministers, who are focused on converting others and winning souls for Christ cannot follow the higher path. They are stuck at a lower level, and they will not free themselves from the consciousness of using force for they are seeking to convert others through force.

The true way to convert others is that you walk the path to Christhood and you free your consciousness from the elements of anti-christ whereby you become the open door for the universal Christ consciousness to express itself through you. This expression of Christ may convert those who are ready to be converted. Believing that you have to convert everybody to the membership of an outer religion and that this will please Christ is a complete fallacy. It does nothing for *me* or my work to raise the consciousness of humankind. It only keeps *you* trapped in the consciousness of using force.

There are so many subtle elements of this force-based consciousness that are driving the Christian religion today. They are subtle, some of them very, very subtle. You will have to be willing to look at each and every one of them and transcend them if you are to reform Christianity and turn it into the kind of movement that I desired to start and that I desire to see today.

How could Christians justify violence?

Let me begin by pointing to some of the more obvious examples of the force-based consciousness. The first one is the undeniable fact that in the history of the Christian religion there has been a fair amount of physical violence. There was the attempt to forcefully suppress other religions that started almost as soon as Christianity became the official religion of the Roman Empire. There was the forceful burning of books and the removal of any alternative sources of knowledge, be it the Greek philosophers or anything else. There was the massacre of the Cathars, other acts of the Inquisition, the Crusades, the persecution of scientists, the war between Protestants and Catholics, other wars enacted by the Catholic Church to conquer territory and take political control, the witch hunts and numerous other undeniable acts of physical violence.

You have to be in a state of complete denial in order to ignore or sweep away the significance of this. If you are to ever change Christianity, you will need to be willing to honestly look at this and ask yourself how it was possible that the Christian religion could commit physical violence and feel that this was justified by Christ. You will have to acknowledge that this was only possible because the Christian religion had been taken over, not only by the consciousness of anti-christ in a general sense but by specific people who were embodying the consciousness of anti-christ to an ultimate degree. They were acting as the marionettes for disembodied beings in the emotional realm, and even for the beings in the mental and identity realms.

If you will not acknowledge the existence of the consciousness of anti-christ and the forces of anti-christ – and that some people have embodied this – then you cannot reform the Christian religion for they will continue to exert their influence even today. Those are the false pastors, those wolves in sheep's clothing, who appear beautiful outwards, but inwards they are like whitened sepulchers filled with dead men's bones.

Today, many Christians will say that *their* church has risen above the level of committing physical violence in terms of killing other people. There are still many churches, for example in the United States, who felt it was justified, that it was doing God's work, to go to war in Iraq. Even though these Christians washed their hands of the actual act of killing, they were condoning it. As I said, if you lust after your neighbor's wife, you have already committed adultery with her in your mind. If you condone that your government goes to war, you have committed an act of war in your mind. You have done to yourself what you want your government to do to others.

Let us just consider that most Christian churches and most Christians would not directly commit acts of physical violence. Let us acknowledge that this is progress, this is a raising of the collective consciousness of these congregations and churches. Let us now consider more subtle acts of violence.

What would you consider concerning the pedophilia scandal in the Catholic Church? Taking advantage of your position as a Catholic priest and raping an innocent child, is that not an act of violence? How is it possible that a modern church in today's age can have this kind of violence happen on a systematic, large-scale basis? How is it possible that this church for decades systematically covered it up, instead of protecting the innocent children?

The institution attempted to protect itself by moving pastors from one parish to another, thereby essentially enabling them to keep on abusing children who had no protection. They knew not that it was a wolf in sheep's clothing who had come to their parish. They trusted that particular priest because he was sent there by the church that they had been brought up never to question under the threat of going to hell. Is this not violence of the worst order; not only *physical* but *psychological* violence?

A fear-based approach to "salvation"

What shall we say of the many churches, especially the fundamentalist kind, who keep their entire congregations in a lifelong state of fear? These people have questions about life, about the spiritual side of life, but they barely dare acknowledge their questions. They are so afraid that if they question the doctrines of their church, if they question the literal interpretation of their pastor, if they ask questions that their pastor cannot answer, then they will go to hell, an eternity of torment in hell.

Yes, this may not be physical violence, but is it not psychological violence? In my vision, the undivided vision of the Christ mind, it *is* violence. I am perfectly aware that the mind of anti-christ can come up with any amount of arguments – subtle, sophisticated, intellectual arguments – for why is it necessary to scare people with hell in order to get them to reform themselves and avoid sin, in order to get them to reform themselves and avoid actually going to this hell.

You will *not* be saved by conforming to an outer church and an outer doctrine. Neither will you, for that matter, be condemned to hell for not doing so. Hell is more than anything a state of consciousness. It is a collective downward spiral of energy that takes over your mind. Hell is what you experience on a constant basis in your own mind. Yes, there are, as I said, places in the emotional realm that are very similar to an outer hell, but the only thing that can attract you there is your own state of consciousness. When you indulge in a certain state of consciousness for several lifetimes on earth, you can magnetize yourself to one of these hell holes in the emotional realm. This is again the result of your own choices and your own state of consciousness, not that you are condemned there by God or by Christ.

I do not judge based on the dualistic consciousness of antichrist. I judge righteous judgment based on the unified vision of the Christ mind that sees the oneness of all life. I do not send anyone to hell, nor does Saint Peter. He is not even an ascended master, having not been willing, to this day, to let go of the Peter consciousness, the denial of the Christ in himself. There is no one up here in heaven who sits there and sends people to hell. We only seek to help people raise their consciousness. Of course, we cannot help all people. Those who will not look at the beam in their own eye, we are not able to help. We must allow them to magnetize themselves to whatever environment will help them outplay their state of consciousness to such an extreme degree that they finally have had enough and ask for deliverance.

You may know that certain people become addicted to alcohol or drugs and that some of them have to go into a downward spiral until things become so bad that they hit bottom and cry out for help. What actually happens in this process is that they finally become willing to look at themselves and see: "I am the one who has to change, not the rest of the world." Only when you are willing to change yourself, can we actually help you. Until then, you must be allowed to act out your free-will choices to the degree that is necessary for you to turn around.

This is precisely what is happening in many Christian churches. People have entered into a fear-based state of consciousness. They have started worshiping the idol of the external God, the angry God in the sky, and the external Christ. They have put themselves beyond our help, and we must allow them to outplay this consciousness until they are so fed up with this fear-based approach to life that they finally cry out for deliverance and say: "How can I change myself? I now see that *I* am the one who has to change."

15 | THE SUPPRESSION OF WOMEN IN CHRISTIANITY

There are many of these subtle aspects of the force-based consciousness, but there is one that I particularly want to draw to the attention of those who are willing to renew the Christian religion. There is no greater, no more devastating, act of physical and psychological violence in the history of the Christian religion than the suppression and putting down of women. This suppression of women has been going on for eons on this planet. It was entirely engineered by the fallen beings, the false teachers.

They knew very well how the consciousness of antichrist works by creating two polarities. Their strategy has always been to divide and conquer. They seek to divide all human beings in their own minds so that they are houses divided against themselves. They also seek to create outer divisions between nationalities, ethnic groups, religions, political affiliations. Just look at this planet and see how many of these outer divisions there are. The very basic division created by the fallen beings is the division based on the design of your physical bodies, namely the division between men and women.

Women did not cause the fall of man

One of the reasons these fallen beings had to eradicate the belief in reincarnation was that when you accept reincarnation, you realize that the soul that reincarnates is neither male nor female; it is androgynous. A soul can actually take on both a male and a female body. Some souls will embody in the same sex for many lifetimes; others will switch, sometimes quite often. When you acknowledge this fact, you realize that it is necessary to reinterpret Genesis once again. The version of the Genesis story that you have been handed down through the Jewish religion is in fundamental ways affected by the fallen beings, the false teachers. You will even see this in the fact that there are two creation stories in Genesis. One says that God said: Let us make man in our own image, after our own likeness and let them have dominion over the earth. The other says that man is created out of the dust of the earth. Well, which one is it? Are you a spiritual being, created in a higher realm in the image and likeness of your Creator and then sent into a physical body on earth? Or are you a material being created out of the dust, the energy, of the material universe? If you are honest and read Genesis carefully, you will see that these two stories cannot be reconciled, at least not without some convoluted, fancy, intellectual reasoning.

The deeper reality is that Adam and Eve do not represent a male human being and a female human being. They represent two aspects of your own being. They represent the fact that you have a spiritual aspect of your being, which is pure awareness, namely what I have called the Conscious You, and then you have a soul, which is the vehicle you use to express yourself in the material world.

Originally, the Conscious You was created as an extension of God's being and sent into the material world. You then, over many lifetimes, built the soul vehicle. When you started going into the consciousness of separation and duality, you started creating a soul vehicle out of the dust of the earth, the dust of the dualistic state of consciousness. Today, you are a composite being. You still have the Conscious You, which is the core of your identity. It is still as pure as when it was first created. Nothing that has happened to you in this world has stained the Conscious You because it is pure awareness and cannot be affected by anything that happens on earth.

Your soul has indeed been stained by the experiences you have had, including being attacked, killed, tortured, maimed, put down or psychologically tortured by the false teachers, the fallen beings. You have reacted to this over many lifetimes and built a soul vehicle out of the dust of the earth. It has elements of the consciousness of anti-christ in it, and that is the beam in your own eye that you must remove.

The true interpretation, the higher interpretation, of the story of Genesis is that Adam represents the male or spiritual aspect of your being: the Conscious You. Eve represents the female aspect of your being: the soul vehicle. It was the soul vehicle that was vulnerable to the deception of the serpent. What happened was that you fell into separation, you created the ego, and then this ego has now set itself up as a god, knowing good and evil, *defining* what is good and evil in your own vision.

Blaming women for the fall is an evil plot

Adam has chosen to fall with Eve, to fall with the soul, in order to redeem the soul or the energies of the soul. You do this by walking the path of Christhood, but you are not thereby redeeming the soul or the ego. You are walking the path of letting one aspect at the time die so that you are reborn of fire and returning to your original state of pure awareness where you have left behind your nets. You are not simply leaving the soul. You recognize that you created the soul and that you are responsible for your use of God's creative energy. It is up to you to restore the balance of the universe by redeeming the energy that makes up your soul vehicle. You do this by raising its vibration, by freeing it from the thought matrix that keeps it trapped in a lower vibration, the thought matrix that springs from the lies of anti-christ. This is the path, the *true* path, of Christ.

That is why I said to Nicodemus that no man has ascended back to heaven save he that descended from heaven. The soul vehicle can never ascend to heaven. Only the Conscious You that descended from heaven can ascend back, and it does so when it stops identifying itself with the soul vehicle, when it has reconstituted the energies that make up the soul vehicle and when it has dismissed the lies of anti-christ that generated the soul vehicle.

When you let the final aspect of the soul vehicle die on the cross where you, the Conscious You, have been crucified, when you give up that last ghost, *then* you can ascend. When you understand this deeper reality of Christ, you see that it is a complete dis-interpretation of Genesis to blame those who are embodied in a female body for the Fall of Man. It simply is not true that *women* caused the fall of *man*.

This is a deliberate fallacy, engineered by the false teachers of this world and spread through the three monotheistic religions of Judaism, Christianity and Islam. It is a deliberate ploy to divide humankind in a most fundamental way by making those who happen to be in a male body in this lifetime feel superior to those who are in a female body in this lifetime. It is an extremely divisive, subversive plot of division. It is evil at its very core. If you are to reform Christianity into a true movement for Christ, it must be rooted out to its very core.

Jesus denounces the suppression of women

When I walked the earth in a physical body, I did not put down women whatsoever. There are various alternative gospels that even document this. I attempted to raise women up, but I was limited by the cultural context in which I appeared. There was only so much that could be said back then about the need to raise up women and to remove the burden.

If Christianity had taken the foundation that I set and had multiplied the talents, then Christianity would, over these past 2,000 years, have been a force for the liberation of women. Instead, it was taken over by the exact same fallen beings that had created the division in the first place. Therefore, Christianity became an instrument for putting down women even more than they were before.

If you think this is to my liking, you are severely mistaken. It is time to publicly state – in a way that people can physically read and therefore cannot deny – that I, the ascended Jesus Christ, completely denounce the putting down of women in Christianity. I denounce it in the most powerful way it can possibly be done. It is an abomination to me and it needs to stop— *and it needs to stop right now!*

May those who have ears to hear, hear and may they *act!* This is the greatest burden that prevents the reform of Christianity. Those who deny this – those Christian leaders who insist on sitting in their citadels of power and continue the policy that suppresses women – they have no part with me. Their minds are taken over by the consciousness of anti-christ, by the forces of anti-christ or they are themselves incarnations of the very false teachers, of the fallen beings. I do not care what position they hold in Christianity. I hereby denounce them all.

It is all well and good that you have a Pope who claims to be humble and wants to serve the poor. But has he done anything to raise up women in the Catholic Church? Nay! Therefore, has he done anything to correct the most severe problem in the Christian religion? Nay, he has not!

There should be no position in any Christian church that could not be held by women. If the Catholic Church was ever reformed according to my directives, it should be possible for a woman to become Pope if she was qualified. It should be possible for women to be priests and to be bishops.

The celibacy fallacy

This would mean that you would have to get rid of this completely artificial claim that priests should be celibate. This is complete nonsense. It is completely against my desires.

I have talked about a higher and a lower path of Christ. The lower path are for those who are not ready to go within and seek oneness with me. There needs to be priests who can minister to these people, and these priests need to know what these people are going through.

One of the great challenges for all people is their relationships. How can a priest council his flock in terms of relationships if he is not in a relationship and does not know anything about the dynamics of being in a relationship?

There should be priests who are married and know what the congregation is dealing with. It may be perfectly valid that there are those who are either priests or have other positions in churches who choose to live a celibate lifestyle and focus on the inner path. This should not be a mandate by the institution but an individual choice.

15 | The Suppression of Women in Christianity

The two basic creative polarities

There are so many ways in which women are put down and treated as secondary beings, but I tell you that in the spiritual realm there is no putting down of women or of the female element for we recognize the deeper reality. I have said that the consciousness of anti-christ has two divisions that are opposites, but you must recognize that the consciousness of anti-christ is always a perversion of the higher reality of the Christ mind.

The higher reality of the Christ mind is that the Creator is one undivided, indivisible being. In order to create anything, the Creator had to create out of its own consciousness and Being. The first act of creation was to create two polarities of its own Being, and these polarities were conscious beings. One is holding what you, from the perspective on earth, would call the male, masculine or outgoing polarity and the other is holding the feminine, female or contracting polarity.

These are the two basic forces of creation, an expanding and a contracting. In order to create any form that can be sustained over time, there must be a balance between the outgoing and the ingoing force, the outbreath and the inbreath of God.

What balances the two forces is the Christ mind, which ensures oneness so that the two polarities remain complementary and do not become opposites. It is when you step into the consciousness of separation and division that the two basic polarities become opposites that cancel out each other or destroy or break down the forms that are created. This is how the consciousness of anti-christ perverted the two basic forces of creation, using this to create the division between men and women on earth.

Equality between men and women

I have hereby denounced this plot, this lie of the fallen beings, in a physical, public way. Let those who have ears to hear heed these words and let them be willing to act to reform their Christian church so that it is based on total and absolute equality between men and women.

I am, of course, not advocating an Amazonian shift that suddenly elevates women to the position now held by men. I am advocating a complete equality between the sexes, which will not only liberate women but will actually liberate men as well. What have I said: Before you can do onto others, you must have done to yourself. Before you can put down women, you, men, must have put down a part of yourselves, namely the female aspect of your own beings. When you do put down an element of your own being, you cannot have balance. If you cannot have balance, you are a house divided. You will be pulled into the dualistic extremes, and you will find it much more difficult to find a balanced perspective, the narrow way of Christ.

What is the deeper meaning behind my statement that there is a broad way, which is followed by most people, and that there is a straight and narrow path that few people find? The broad way is the divided way where your mind is divided by two dualistic opposites. It is the broad way that has an extension in space; it has two opposite sides. The straight and narrow way is a single line that has no extension.

When you go down a road, it has two sides. When you walk a line, a wire suspended, there is only one line to walk on. It is like walking on a razor's edge. This is the balanced perspective of the Christ mind. Men cannot find it if they put down the feminine aspect of themselves. Women cannot find it if they accept the putting down from men and put down the feminine in themselves or if they suppress the masculine aspect of their own beings.

Both men and women have the male and the female in themselves because all have a Conscious You and all have a soul. What has happened to all people, men and women, is that the soul has set itself up as the master of your house whereas it should be the Father, the Conscious You, that should be the master of your individual household, the household of your mind.

You should be in command, not the soul vehicle. You use the soul vehicle only for expression in this world, and then you seek to free it from the elements that keep you trapped in this world, the elements of anti-christ. This is the correct way to walk the path of Christ.

A new movement to bring balance

I expect that there are tens of thousands of people who will be willing to recognize the validity and the reality of what I am saying. They will be the forerunners for a new movement to act upon this and restore balance between masculine and feminine to Christianity. I expect that millions of others will follow when the forerunners take the first steps.

I know well that some have already started this, and for you my words are simply meant as an encouragement. You are on the right track, but you could benefit from the teachings I have given in this book and elsewhere to accelerate your efforts and have a clear vision of your goal and the means to get there.

I am the ascended Jesus Christ. When I walked the earth 2,000 years ago, I appeared in a male body. Even today, as an ascended master, I present myself as a masculine being, a masculine form. When you ascend, you transcend the divisions into physical sexes that are so dominant on earth. You become, from an earthly perspective, more of an androgynous being who is simply beyond the division into sexes that you see on earth. This means that you also transcend any and all sense of value judgment associated with the physical division into sexes. I have absolutely no value judgment that ranks women lower than men; *none whatsoever.*

Those who claim to be the true followers of Jesus Christ should strive to follow the path whereby you can also raise yourself above this division and this value judgment. These are my teachings on this topic for now. I am sure I shall find occasion to bring forth other teaching as the time and the cycles are right. Enough has been given that you can start the process of restoring women to their rightful place in Christianity.

16 | A MOVEMENT GUIDED BY THE SPIRIT

"Blessed are the meek, for they shall inherit the earth." What might be the deeper meaning behind this statement? What does it mean to be meek? Compare it to what I have given you in this book about those who are trapped in the consciousness of anti-christ and actually believe that they know better than God how the universe works or how it *should* work. They know better than God how self-aware beings should be saved.

I have told you that many of these proud, arrogant beings have embodied as the leaders of the Christian religion, the leaders in the field of science, the leaders in the field of politics. They think they know best, they think they have defined a thought system which is ultimately true. Anything that contradicts it or even goes beyond it, is automatically labeled as untrue, unreal or in other ways invalid. They feel perfectly justified in ignoring it.

Those are the proud, the arrogant. The meek are those who realize that there is more to know than what they already know. Their minds and hearts are open to the potential that a true spiritual teacher, even one embodied or expressed in a form that is somewhat surprising to them, might actually teach them something of value.

The judgment of Christ upon the proud

These are the people who are open to my teaching. They are the ones who shall inherit the earth for the simple reason that every time someone dares to embody the Living Christ, this incarnation brings about the judgment of a certain group of the proud, the arrogant, the fallen beings. When I walked the earth in a physical body 2,000 years ago, there was a certain group of these fallen beings who plotted to kill me. In doing so, they brought about their own judgment. I did not come to judge people; I came that they might be saved and enter the kingdom of God. Those who will not follow my instructions, those who will not let me take them beyond their mental boxes, they will judge themselves by their denial of Christ.

It is, in a certain sense, ironic that the foremost deniers of Christ in the world today are the leaders and members of what they claim to be the Christian religion, the only true representative of Christ on earth. When you actually understand the fallen consciousness and the fallen beings, and how they have influenced planet earth, this really is not surprising.

They will always attempt to ignore the Living Christ in whatever form he embodies. They will attempt to get other people, the population at large, to ignore him. If he will not be ignored, they will kill him. They will kill his followers if they can. If they cannot do that, then they will use it, pervert it, turn it around and use it for their purposes of controlling the population.

There is not much new under the sun for these fallen beings only have limited options. Their options work only because so far the majority of the people on earth have not been willing to awaken and see what is actually going on. They are not willing to see that they have followed the blind leaders. Those who are the meek, those who are open, they *can* and *will* be awakened in this age.

Most Christians will reject this book

I know well what most of the leaders and most of the members of Christian churches will say about this book. Most will attempt to ignore it. If there are enough people who take this book, run with it, talk about it and recommend it to others, then there will come a point where they can no longer ignore it and then they will attempt to denounce it.

They will attempt to denounce the book itself and say that this could not possibly be from the true, the real, Jesus Christ. They will attack the messenger who is bringing forth this book, turn his personal life upside down, inside out and say that such a person could not possibly be worthy to be a messenger for the real, ascended Jesus Christ. Then, they will take the book, twist and turn every sentence, every word, and say that this particular statement is in contradiction with this doctrine of our church and therefore could not possibly be true. The underlying claim will be, of course, that if this book was really from the real Jesus Christ, then it would validate and conform to every doctrine and belief of their particular church.

This is a total denial of Christ. As I have said, the Christ comes into this world to set you free from your mental boxes. It does not matter whether that mental box is a religion that claims to be Christianity and claims to represent Christ on earth. Christ still comes to set you free from *any* mental box that keeps you trapped in this world and keeps you trapped on the false path to salvation because you are following the blind leaders.

Christ challenges all Christian churches

There is no Christian church on earth that I will not challenge. *All* Christian churches on earth have been influenced by the consciousness of anti-christ. I will continue to challenge your illusions until you either awaken yourself, leave your nets and follow me or bring about your own judgment so that you cannot continue to embody on this planet. This is what I have been charged to do by God, and I will carry this through to the finish, to the end of the world, to the end of the reign of the fallen beings on earth. There shall not be one fallen being left in embodiment on earth, in the emotional realm, in the mental realm or in the identity realm when I am done with this earth.

I would remind you of a statement I made 2,000 years ago: "He who denies me before men, him must I deny before the Father." He who denies this book and my Living Word and my living teaching before men, him must I deny before the Father.

This may sound ominous, as if I am sitting up here judging people, but I am not. People are judging themselves by denying this book as an expression of the Living Christ, of the ascended Jesus Christ. You are denying me before men, and if you deny the Living Christ in the material world, how can you follow the Living Christ beyond the material world into my Father's kingdom? By denying Christ in this world, you are denying yourself entry into the spiritual world. Is this really so difficult to see, given what I have explained in this book?

There is nothing ominous about this. I am not an angry judge, sitting in the sky. I am charged with bringing about the salvation of most people on earth, and the judgment of those who will not be saved so that the earth can be purified and raised up to no longer being dominated by the fallen consciousness. I do this by stirring up the waters on earth with my Spirit, with my light, and with an outer teaching when possible.

All people must be saved through Jesus

I am the ascended Jesus Christ. Today, I hold a spiritual office as the Planetary Christ, which is also the Office of the Savior for each and every lifestream embodying on earth.

When I said that: "No man cometh unto the Father, but by me," it has two meanings. The general sense is that no one comes to the Father except by going through the Christ consciousness. You must unify with the universal Christ consciousness until you put on personal Christhood and the Christ becomes individualized through you—in you. The more specific meaning is that there is indeed a spiritual office as the savior for this planet. The office itself is universal. Throughout the ages, it has been held by a number of different ascended beings. For almost 2,000 years, it has been held by me.

Although the Christ consciousness has a universal aspect, I have said that it can be expressed on earth only through an individual being, which means that the Christ becomes individualized through that being. Contrary to what most Christians want to believe, when I walked the earth 2,000 years ago my expression of Christhood was determined by my individuality. There have been other people before me and after me who have expressed some degree of personal Christhood. They have been different from me, they have expressed their Christhood differently from me, and this is perfectly in order.

There is not one expression of Christhood. This is again the false standard of perfection created by the fallen beings. There are innumerable ways to express Christhood in different contexts, in different times, in different societies. The Christ has only one aim, namely that all might have life by absorbing the body and blood of the Christ consciousness, and that they might have it more abundantly by being able to allow the Christ consciousness to express itself through them.

The abundant life is the individual expression of the Christ consciousness through you. This is life, this is abundance: When the Christ, the universal Christ mind, is streaming through your individual mind. When I walked the earth, I expressed my Christhood in an individualized way. It is not the only way it could have been done. It is not the only way it *can* be done; it is not the only way it *will* be done.

This is important for various reasons, but one is that today I am the ascended being who holds the Office of Savior for this planet. I have transcended what many human beings see as individuality because I have transcended the outer mind, the outer personality of the ego and the separate self. I have not transcended the divine individuality that defined me as an individual being to begin with and that I have built on to through my long sojourn in the world of form. Surely, I did not pop up out of nowhere 2,000 years ago on this planet. I have a long history before that embodiment.

Today, the situation is that any human being in embodiment on earth can be saved – can enter the kingdom of God, can ascend from earth – in only one way: by going through the Office of Savior for this planet. That office is held by *me*, which means that you must go through the individual being that I am.

Coming into oneness with Jesus

This first of all means that you must be willing to come into oneness with me as the individualized ascended being that I am. This presents a special challenge, which is actually a very fair challenge.

In order to ascend from earth, you must be willing to let the mortal self, the separate self, die so that you can be reborn. How can you actually do this? You cannot do it by plunging yourself into a vacuum so how do you do it? You do it by coming into oneness with a being who is beyond your individualized self. You are partly coming into oneness with your own higher being, but the requirement, the cosmic law, is that you also come into oneness with an ascended being who serves as your spiritual teacher.

You will recall that the fall into separation, as illustrated by the Garden of Eden story, was the process whereby you turned your back to the spiritual teacher sent by God. The only way to re-enter the kingdom of God is to come back into oneness with the spiritual teacher, and currently the Office of Planetary Christ and Planetary Savior is held by me, the ascended Jesus Christ.

You need to come into oneness with me. Of course, in order to come into oneness with me spiritually, you need to shed your outer images of Christ and your outer images of Jesus. This means that no matter who you are – no matter where you have grown up on this planet, no matter what religion you have followed in this or previous lifetimes – you cannot ascend until you make peace with Jesus Christ. Given that you can hardly grow up on this planet without being exposed to some form of Christianity, this means that you must be willing to shed all of the man-made images to which you have been exposed.

You need to be willing to shed *all* of the images of Jesus Christ, and of Christ as a universal concept, that spring from the consciousness of anti-christ. This applies whether you are Christian or not, whether you grew up in a Christian religion or not. These false images of Christ are very much part of the collective consciousness on earth. In order to ascend, you must transcend all aspects of the collective consciousness. More than that, you must go through the office that I hold. In order to come into oneness with me, you must shed all of the images that cause you to relate to me from a distance.

How do you come into oneness with me? You must stand "naked" before me so that you do not look at me through any images. You see me as I am, and then you can come into oneness with me. As long as you hold on to an image of me defined on earth or in the material world, you are relating to me through that image. You are seeing me as outside yourself, as separate from yourself, as distant from yourself. This is not oneness, this can never be oneness.

The meek shall inherit the earth for they shall be willing to start challenging and questioning the mental images that are restricting them. They are restricting the expression of their own individual creativity but also restricting their relationship to God and to Christ. Those who love father or mother or brother or sister more than me are not worthy of me. This means that if there is anything here on earth, including a graven image of me, that you think is more important than coming into oneness with me, then you are not ready to open yourself up to oneness. You are not ready to leave your nets and follow me unconditionally. If you are not ready for this, you cannot be part of the movement to renew Christianity, to reinvent Christianity.

How to renew Christianity

There are people who will be able to sense the authority with which I speak in this book, yet some of them will think that what they have to do is follow what I have said in this book to the letter and interpret it literally. Some will think they now have to elevate this messenger to the status of some kind of authority figure who can tell them how to reconstruct the Christian religion. This is not what I have in mind, neither is it what the messenger desires.

What I desire is in no way to repeat the errors of the Christian religion. What was the greatest error of the Christian religion? It was the formation of one centralized church, the Roman Catholic Church, which used force to suppress all other forms of Christianity if at all possible. What happened in this process was that the Comforter, the Holy Spirit, the individualized expression of Christ, was shut out of Christianity and it has remained shut out to this day.

I have no desire to create a new centralized church that would supposedly be the only true church of Jesus Christ. I have a desire to see many individual initiatives, movements, churches and sects that are based on one or more people walking the path of individual Christhood until they attain some degree of oneness with me.

This is already happening to some degree. There are indeed people who have some position in some Christian churches and movements who have inner attunement with me. There is no one who could not benefit from more consciously walking the path of individual Christhood. There are many more who have the potential to attain inner attunement with me, but who have not yet dared to acknowledge or dared to express this in their lives.

I have said, in one of my previous books through this messenger [*The Mystical Teachings of Jesus*] that there are 10,000 people in embodiment who are ready to acknowledge, very quickly, that they have attained some degree of Christhood in past lives. These people are ready to begin expressing it and could very quickly rise to the point of daring to express it. I have said that there are millions more who are ready to follow the path of individual Christhood so that in this lifetime they can claim and express their Christhood.

This does not mean that all of these millions of people will become members of one organization that is centralized around some person with ultimate authority. It means that the ultimate authority in their lives will be the Christ within, the Comforter, the Holy Spirit, their direct attunement with me, the ascended Jesus Christ, or another ascended master.

I desire to see a living movement where there is room for individual expression, but it comes from the one spirit, the Holy Spirit, the Christ Spirit. This is the movement I desire to see. I am fully capable of working with millions of people at the same time. I am not looking for a church that is outwardly perfect. I am looking for churches and organizations and movements that help the members transcend themselves, transcend their present state of consciousness and rise higher and higher towards individual Christhood. This can be done in many different ways. In fact, it *must* be done in many different ways for people are at many different levels of consciousness and come from many different backgrounds.

A diversified movement

Do you not see that there is a need for a diversified movement so that people, no matter what mental box they are currently trapped in, can find some movement that can help them start where they are and take one step at a time towards personal Christhood? It is not a matter of having some centralized doctrine; it is a matter of recognizing that you must start where people are at in consciousness and offer them something that can take them from that point and one step higher—then another step, and another, and another.

Surely, as people move closer and closer to Christhood, they will begin to feel more and more unified. They will be able to see beyond their outer differences and come into a sense of inner oneness. This could eventually develop into some centralized structure where people from different movements and churches work together. This is something that will emerge spontaneously from the spirit and not because some emperor or other potentate on earth decides to create the "one true church."

If you disagree with points in this book

I know well that those who are open to this book will have read up to this point because they felt there was something here that spoke to them, that spoke to their hearts. I know also that most people will have certain issues and statements that I have brought up with which they find it difficult to agree. This may be because you still have certain illusions created by the mind of anti-christ that are so deeply ingrained in your mind that you have not yet questioned them and let them go. It may also be because you are meant to express Christhood in a way that is different from the way it is expressed here.

I have had other people in the past who were able to bring forth a teaching that came directly from me. Many of these messengers have thought that the way I expressed myself through them was the only way that I *could* express myself. Many people believe that if I am one being, sitting up here in the spiritual realm, then there should be only one truth I could bring forth on earth and there should be only one authoritative way that I could do this. I have attempted to explain in this book that this is precisely the projection of the fallen mindset. There are many other ways that I could express myself through human beings in embodiment. It is simply a matter of which audience I am seeking to reach. I will adapt my expression to their level of consciousness so that I can reach them where they are at and help them rise higher.

You might feel that there are certain things about the way I am expressing myself in this book that do not fully resonate with you. Well, then don't waste your time and attention on condemning or criticizing this messenger or telling him how he should take messages from me. Instead, walk the path of individual Christhood, apply yourself so that I can speak through *you*. Be careful that you are willing to remove all mental images of me before you claim that you can be a better messenger than someone else. Be careful to realize that as long as you are comparing yourself to others, as long as you are criticizing or putting down another, you have not freed yourself from the mental images that will either prevent me from expressing myself through you or that might even color the expression to some degree.

I have in the past had to express myself through messengers who were not neutral and who therefore did color the message to some degree. We have to work with what is available to us, but what I would like to see is people who have realized what I have said in this book and who have made it a goal for themselves to become the open door for the ascended Jesus Christ.

Being the open door for Christ

You do realize, do you not, that a door is fully open only when there is nothing obstructing the flow of light through it? You will know that there are some doors that may have colored glass. Light can shine through it, but what comes through is colored by the glass. I desire those who will dedicate their lives to becoming fully open doors.

I have given teachings in this book, I have given many other teachings through this messenger, that can help you attain this status. Again, I have no desire and he has no desire to set him up as an ultimate authority. But it needs to be stated that he has been a sufficiently open door that I have been able to bring forth teachings that have value for a very large number of the people who have the potential to put on Christhood in this lifetime. You may not agree with everything and you don't have to agree with everything. What you have to recognize here is that there is enough material, and it is pure enough, that you can use it to transcend your own mental images and bring yourself to the point of being an open door for the ascended Jesus Christ, or for other ascended masters as is in your individual divine plan.

I am not hereby saying that all those who read this book need to go out and openly declare that they are messengers for the ascended masters or for the ascended Jesus Christ. I am not looking for all who accept this book to necessarily speak openly about this. There are many different roles to play, there are many who could be pastors or leaders of churches and movements without taking direct messages but still having the inner attunement whereby they are led by the spirit and not by any of the false spirits, the fallen spirits.

This is the potential, the only realistic potential, for renewing the Christian religion and bringing it into alignment with the true teachings of the ascended Jesus Christ that I am. It will not happen through a centralized authority on earth. It will happen only through the flow of the spirit, the flow of the universal Christ consciousness, through the individual minds of those who have chosen to become the open doors that no man and no woman can shut.

Deny me if you will. Use your sophisticated arguments to say that because of this or that point, this or that statement, this could not possibly be genuine. Deny me if you will. Whether you deny me or accept me, I will have accomplished my purpose of forcing you to either go up or go down. If you go up in Christhood, you will help raise this planet up. If you go down by denying Christ, then you will bring about your own judgment. You will be removed from this planet, and this will also help the planet be raised up to a higher level. Either way, my purpose will be fulfilled.

My purpose is to bring forth a teaching in this age that is the culmination of what I started 2,000 years ago. I said back then: "I have yet many things to say unto you, but you cannot bear them now." I have said many of these things through this messenger and through other messengers. I intend to say many more things through this and other messengers as people make themselves willing and ready to receive it.

I am indeed the ascended Jesus Christ, and I intend to fulfill the promise I made 2,000 years ago: "I am with you always even unto the end of the world." This does not mean that the world will cease to exist, but it does mean that it will cease to exist in the twilight zone that allows the fallen consciousness to be in control of this planet.

The end of the world is the end of the reign of the fallen beings and the raising of the earth to where it will be reigned by Christed beings in embodiment. To this cause I am fully committed! *Are you with me?*

About the Author

Kim Michaels is an accomplished writer and author, having published more than 40 books. He has conducted spiritual conferences and workshops in 14 countries, has counseled hundreds of spiritual students and has done numerous radio shows on spiritual topics. Kim has been on the spiritual path since 1976. He has studied a wide variety of spiritual teachings and practiced many techniques for raising consciousness. For personal information, visit Kim at *www.KimMichaels.info*.

From the Heart of Jesus, vol 1

The teachings in this book have helped hundreds of thousands of people gain a deeper appreciation for Jesus's teachings about the mystical path that he taught 2,000 years ago and that he still teaches today—for those who are able to make an inner connection with him.

TODAY MANY PEOPLE CANNOT find a lasting heart connection to the real Jesus and his teachings because, according to most Christian churches, Jesus no longer talks to us. In reality, Jesus is a spiritual being and he is working to help all people who are able to raise their consciousness and attune to his Presence. For the past 2,000 years he has maintained a line of communication through those who have been willing to serve as messengers for his Living Word and who have pursued an understanding of his true message instead of settling for official Christian doctrines.

In this book, the ascended Jesus reveals the mystical teachings that he gave to his most advanced disciples. He explains why his true teachings are as relevant today as they were two millennia ago and how you can develop a personal relationship with him—one of the most remarkable spiritual teachers of all time.

Once you admit that mainstream religious traditions have not answered your questions about life, it is truly liberating to read the deep and meaningful answers in this book. Encouraging, moving and profound, this enlightening book will help you attain inner attunement with Jesus, even mystical union with him.

You will learn how to:
- recognize the silent, inner voice of Christ in your heart
- achieve permanent inner peace and happiness by getting connected with the Christ Consciousness
- heal yourself from emotional wounds
- get guidance from Jesus, who is your greatest teacher and friend
- communicate directly with Jesus

From the Heart of Jesus, vol 2

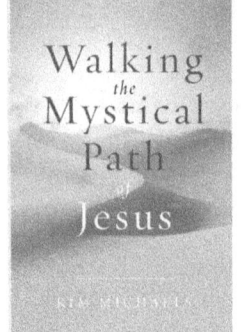

The teachings in this book have helped hundreds of thousands of people gain a deeper appreciation for the mystical path that Jesus taught to his disciples 2000 years ago, the path towards union with God, a state of mind beyond most people's highest dreams.

TODAY MANY PEOPLE HAVE trouble discovering the small, easy and practical steps towards a state of consciousness that is beyond human conflicts and pitfalls. In this book the ascended master Jesus describes how to start walking the mystical path that will eventually restore our most natural ability: the direct experience of God within ourselves.

This book empowers you to discover your personal path and make steady progress towards peace of mind and an inner, mystical experience of God.

Inspiring and profound, this enlightening book contains questions and answers that are easy to read and that help you walk the mystical path of Jesus.

You will learn how to:

- Use the cosmic mirror to speed up your growth
- Get out of old reactionary patterns
- Become free from difficult situations and guilt
- Control your mind
- Leave behind a painful past
- Open your heart to the flow of love from within
- Heal the wounds in your psychology

From the Heart of Jesus, vol 3

Hundreds of thousands of people have been inspired and uplifted by the profound teachings released in the form of conversations between the ascended master Jesus and Kim Michaels.

IN THIS BOOK JESUS DESCRIBES in a very personal way the more advanced stages of the mystical or spiritual path. Jesus describes through practical examples how our souls get fragmented in different embodiments and how the pieces of the soul get lost when we have experienced deep traumas in this lifetime or during previous lifetimes. The result is that our souls become vulnerable to different soul diseases that reduce our ability to enjoy life fully. Jesus explains how to restore our most natural ability—the ability to communicate with God directly. He skillfully explains how to make completely free choices in a world that seems to be full of toxic emotions and attitudes: fear, pride and guilt. Jesus explains how to overcome the sharpest tool of the dualistic mind—doubt combined with fear and pride.

In an easy to read question and answer form, Jesus guides you to a deeper understanding of how some lifestreams are young and mature, some rebel against God and some seek union with God. He helps you break through the opposition from both outside forces and the inner enemy of the ego.

You will learn how to:
- make use of your closest spiritual teacher – Jesus – on your own mystical path
- turn your past traumatic soul experiences into a forward step
- restore the fragments of your soul and by doing this developing your own direct union with God
- learn from even false teachers and overcome fear, pride and doubt
- avoid being disappointed by spiritual organizations
- create a new identity based on love

www.ingramcontent.com/pod-product-compliance
Lightning Source LLC
Chambersburg PA
CBHW021148160426
43194CB00007B/740